CANDY JAR BOOKS · CARDIFF
2024

The right of Jill Curzon to be identified as the Author of the Work has been asserted by her in accordance with the Copyright, Designs and Patents Act 1988.

Printed and bound in the UK by
4edge, 22 Eldon Way, Hockley, Essex, SS5 4AD

ISBN: 978-1-917022-04-0

Published by
Candy Jar Books
Mackintosh House
136 Newport Road, Cardiff, CF24 1DJ
www.candyjarbooks.co.uk

All rights reserved.
No part of this publication may be reproduced, stored in a retrieval system, or transmitted at any time or by any means, electronic, mechanical, photocopying, recording or otherwise without the prior permission of the copyright holder. This book is sold subject to the condition that it shall not by way of trade or otherwise be circulated without the publisher's prior consent in any form of binding or cover other than that in which it is published.

INTRODUCTION
JILL CURZON BY DEREK PARTRIDGE

JILL PLANTEROSE and I met when I was a junior account executive and she was a secretary at Colman Prentis & Varley, an international advertising agency in London. While at CPV, Jill appeared as 'the guilty party' in an Amplex deodorant ad on all the buses and Underground trains in London. I was the 'very important person' in the British Army's recruiting campaign.

We married on February 8th, 1958, at a registry office in Epsom and had a reception at the famous mansion in Nonsuch Park, Cheam, Surrey. Jill was three years younger than me. She became a hard worker in my landscape gardening company, Partridge & Wilcox, Ltd.

I introduced Jill to my hobby of international trap shooting (I was a member of the British team) and she became a very good shot, competing in national championships and overseas events. We even spent our honeymoon shooting wood pigeons in Lincolnshire and sent these back on the train to Oxted, where our local butcher picked them up and sold them in his shop.

We worked together in repertory at Tunbridge Wells in Kent, and we once did an exhibition dance at the famous Lido night club in Paris.

When Jill decided to enter showbiz, I came up with her stage name, Jill Curzon (as we had a flat in Mayfair's Curzon Street).

David Croft started her as Norma, the cute, sexy girl next door, in the BBC series *Hugh & I*, before she went on to star in *Daleks' Invasion Earth 2150AD*. I also worked at the Beeb on *Z-Cars,* and in *Dixon of Dock Green*, where I was a doctor known as Kildare of Dock Green. Later, in America, I guest starred in classic *Star Trek*.

After ten happy years of not being really together, we went our separate ways but remained friends and stayed in touch… for the last fifty-six years.

FOREWORD

WHEN DOES the illusion of life change to reality? I should imagine at the moment when a single event greatly changes one's perception. In my case, upon my learning that I was adopted. Did this information make me less real and, if so, who is the real me? Was it this illusion of my real being that inspired me to venture into the world of stage and screen?

Life isn't, of course, quite that easily explained. Fate being fickle leaves you to decide much of how your life progresses. At least it does so in a teasing way, for it gives you the impression that it is you who makes the decisions that guide your path through life.

Oh, what pleasure it would be to confront Fate and her companion Fortune and ask them what amused or interested them as they watched my unsteady progress from childhood to the woman who never stopped growing.

When during my adolescence I first put pen to diary pages, I had my reasons for doing so. Indeed, there are many reasons for using a diary to record one's progress, with the best being a healthy interest in oneself. Penning prose helps you to put yourself in the third person; it also assists in looking back and looking forward.

By the time I first pulled my diary to my lap I was in my

early teens and so it was blank pages of my life's beginnings that I committed to paper.

Of the many reasons for one keeping a diary, my purpose was based simply on pragmatism. In a sense, back then I considered doing so an unwelcome intrusion. I was so busy living my life, but I often had to remind myself of the necessity to mark and milestone my progress, rather than it being just a distraction. Instinctively, I realised that doing so was an investment, and now as I look back through the turned pages, I know I was subconsciously making decisions that would affect my future.

Self-discipline was my faithful helmsman. Each day I dutifully set down what I considered to be important to me and my budding career as a thespian. Consciously, I realised that, by setting out a record of life's pivotal moments, my recorded map would offer a time-machine record of the places I had visited and the people I had met. The realist side of me suggested that there would be times in the future when my past experiences and those who were to touch upon my life would be a great help as I made my steady and occasionally unsteady progress through what was I supposed would be a colourful life ahead of me.

Uppermost in my determination to succeed was the foreknowledge that we discover, build or discard relationships as we go through life, and for good and bad reasons. Realising from early on that no man is an island I never lost sight of the fact that friends and acquaintances are there to help in the same way that I wanted to offer what I had to help others.

Meticulously, the names and contact details, the places that I visited, and my thoughts and impressions were carefully considered and set down. On each occasion, the entries would be checked, and only when I was finally satisfied would my diary be put to one side. Never once did it occur to me that the most interesting career and varied life was yet to be entered into the still blank pages.

Such was the pragmatism that underscored my resolution to keep my diaries. At some point, the thought occurred to me that the colour I was pursuing in life was already turning into a rainbow.

I concede that fate and fortune proved to be wonderful companions. You see, learning never stops but unfortunately neither does the sand as it trickles and sometimes cascades quickly through the hourglass.

Self-assured and ambitious, driven not so much by the quest for fame but to find myself and to push my capabilities to their limits, the need arose for me to move on from merely keeping a record of names and places. If there are rainbows in your sky, then for goodness' sake, why not describe the colours, and so my diaries metamorphosed into a record of unfolding events.

I was no longer following where the dots might lead. My diaries were now colouring books. Is there a sense of satisfaction with the outcome, now the sand in the hourglass is mostly in the base?

At this point, there is no need for me to consider the pros and cons of keeping a diary. Here, at whatever chapter I find myself in, it confirms the belief I had in myself was well-founded. When one relies on memory it can be as faulty as many judgements made. It is tempting and far too easy to think of life as you think it was rather than come to terms with reality. Am I not right in saying that the diary is the only book that does not lie unless you lie to it?

Of course, there were chances missed, some by a mere hair's breadth. But far better the fickleness of fate than the mind-numbing boredom of a diary written, diligently penned and kept when there is little of interest to fill its pages. I wanted my diary to reflect colour, vitality rather than the tedium of life. I suppose I held the view that, as we live just the once, then surely it is best to live it in a way that once is enough.

Do I count my blessings or ponder on what might have been? It is a delicate balancing act. I have no complaints. It is clear to me that sliding down my rainbow's downward curve my name is still known to so many and I hope for all the right reasons. I was an actress who gave her all and who was indeed the part she played. I am sure the same can be said of so many of my contemporaries and friends like Roger Moore, David Jason and Susannah York.

Being a realist, I know that not everyone avidly absorbs television drama and fewer people than we would like to visit the cinema. For this reason, it is gratifying to know that the many television and theatre drama series I was privileged to play my part in are still remembered many diaries on. This is no mean feat when it is remembered that each year nearly five hundred new television dramas are introduced and screened.

There was in the 1950s much rivalry and jostling for position in the television ratings. We won't at this point even talk about the competing silver screen movies that were keeping audiences queuing at the box offices. Amongst our competition, the best from America were *Bonanza*, *Dragnet*, *The Beverly Hillbillies*, *I Love Lucy*, *The Dick Van Dyke Show*, and *Bewitched*. Yes, all were a hard act to follow. With David Jacobs I served on the panel of *Juke Box Jury*. And my first series was *Hugh and I* with Terry Scott and Hugh Lloyd.

I know I am not alone in doubting if any of the post-millennium television productions, despite the assistance of much more advanced technology, will be as fondly recalled as the great dramas and comedies of the 1950s and 1960s onward. Our generation of actors was the first to bring live theatre to the living rooms of tens of millions of people. What we did set the benchmark for all future television and movie productions.

We succeeded not because we were special but because the viewers for us were special. To us, they were very much part of the show too, especially in comedy, and for this reason, our viewers identified with us and the roles we played. This is the essence of acting and, for me, it is far better than the annual gratuitous backslapping of industry awards. The former is reality while the latter is marketing and there is a world of difference between the two.

As I awaken each morning the senses appear as buds opening and slowly blossoming. One's first levels of alertness might be the aromas of the sub-tropical plants. These sensations will be followed by an awareness of birdsong and finally one's eyes open to make sense of the day ahead. Only then is everything in harmony. How many times have I tried in vain to capture the tranquillity of the ever-changing colours in my oil paintings of the beautiful sea outside my bedroom window, that offers the imagination a panoramic tapestry like no other?

With a minimum of effort, my awakening causes me to smile at the tropical palms that, in the light breeze, appear to wave good morning to me. Against the backdrop of the white stucco wall surrounding my terraces, the bright red geraniums and bougainvillea prepare for their day's sunbathing. The only arresting sight is the female blackbird that in complete disdain of my good taste disturbs the soil in my flowerpots and in doing so scatters soil here and there. But the bird is only having a bath, I think to myself. I'll have mine later!

There will never be a better moment than one's waking moments to reflect on one's good fortune. Other than the birdsong one melody that soothes me is that of the renowned Louis Armstrong, known as Satchmo, the gifted musician who charmed the world with the ballad, 'What a Wonderful World'.

As the sea breeze wafts the lace curtains adorning my bedroom windows I idly wonder if the ballad's composers, Bob Thiele and George Weiss, had been inspired by such a setting as I awake to each morning.

During such idle moments I have a little time to ask how I arrived at this part of my life with a basket filled with such blessings. Not to be taken for granted are such surroundings, my lifestyle, and my having someone to share it with. In my case, being with Leo, who also appreciates the balance between man's ingenuity and hard work, in harmony with the natural environment.

Leo is the love of my life and my rock, without whom my journey through breast cancer in 2005 would have been very different.

My life has been richly peppered, as I diligently took many different avenues, byways that ended as cul-de-sacs or converged.

My daydreams were accompanied by impatience and sometimes intolerance of situations I had little control over.

For all of the pitfalls of life, it is far better to become acquainted with the lure of chance, fate and fortune. Most important of all is realising that you have the gift and ability but only if you have the enthusiasm can you fulfil it.

The blissful world I see through my bedroom window is not shared by everyone in the world. Part of my good fortune was the result of my inheriting my father's house, enabling me to buy our flat.

As I enjoy my awakening reveries the memories flood back and again are relished. And I believe that we all have a path already planned for our lives and ask God for guidance every day to know which way to turn at the crossroads I meet. I am a people person and like the Barbra Streisand song says, 'People who need people are the luckiest people in the world'.

There have been so many friends who cannot easily be compartmentalised. Many friends, associates and fellow travellers like passing ships in the night. There are through life many hands to be shaken and others to be taken according to whim or circumstance.

The term friend is perhaps the most ambiguous word of all. Fate guides friends to us according to their need or our needs and in special cases the needs of both.

Certainly, there will be lovers, and it is no coincidence that the words 'lover' and 'lesson' both start with the same letter. Naturally, most friends are platonic, and acquaintances often become business or career partners due to their being focused on mutual opportunities. With much to share, such partnerships are all part of life's rich tapestry, interwoven with fate.

As a little girl, I always recall being lost in my dreams staring at the distant and often obscure horizons, beyond which were doors to be opened. What lay behind the skylines was waiting to be discovered by me.

My attitude to life whatever happens:
LOVE, LAUGH, and BE GRATEFUL

CHAPTER ONE
EARLY BEGINNINGS

THE ONE thing I was certain of was that the world was not going to come and open my door. This was a door that only I could go through if I chose to turn the handle and to venture inside.

To make a start, one of course needs a bicycle. When I was seven years old, I was gifted my first bike, with hard rubber tyres without air in them. What was there to do but to put my newly acquired bicycle to good use? Before setting out, my first destination of note was the family kitchen in our home in Cheam, Surrey. The railway cuttings were the same railway cuttings so often referred to by the great comedian Tony Hancock.

In the kitchen, and after preparing a sandwich to keep body and soul, I mounted my bicycle. Then unobserved, with my dress and hair curls flying in the breeze, I pedalled off in the direction of London. The great city was only twelve-miles away so I was quite certain I would be there in no time at all.

As my parents had often driven along this same route, I knew the direction I needed to go, down a busy bypass situated not far from our home. Of course, there was a childish vagueness about how long it would take me to reach London but that was hardly a pressing matter. My first lesson in exploring the world was admittedly ill-fated. I had barely made it to the end of the two-mile stretch of highway when I decided that I had bitten off more than I could chew, so me and my sandwich returned home.

During my absence, I hadn't been missed. Back in those days, a child could freely roam without fear or causing alarm. However, a lesson had been learned. I had at least been tested, if not to the full then to the spirit of things yet to come.

CHAPTER TWO
THE CLOUDS OF WAR

MY SCHOOLING was at its earliest stages and those years were some of the happiest of my life. I was born on 29th September 1938, just eleven months before the outbreak of World War II. For such reason, my earliest memories were of radical change, confusion and blacked-out windows on pain of dire punishment. The window coverings in our homes would, with any luck, make the populated regions below appear to be empty countryside to the crews of approaching German aircraft. These blackout curtains were normally made from black cotton material and carefully placed in position at twilight. Then, as soon as it was daybreak these unattractive window shrouds were taken down and folded before being put away by mother.

From 1939, everything one ate was rationed. The rationing started with petrol immediately after the war's outbreak on September 3rd, 1939. From there on, and especially after the German occupation of France in June 1940, basics such as food and clothing were limited by the restrictions of one's ration books. Being a qualified chemist, my mother was conversant with basic things. Eggs being scarce, she preserved those we were able to purchase in a huge bucket filled with brine water. Eggs, if one has the experience can be used in a variety of ways, plus we bought powdered eggs, which were great when scrambled and had a very unique taste.

Meat was scarce and for several years there was very little choice of fare at the butchers and fishmongers. One was obliged to learn to live with minced meat, take it or leave it. The mince lost much of its taste during the boiling. To compensate, Mother did make the most succulent cottage pies, and for occasional change, she cooked delicious shepherd's pies with Lea & Perrins and Oxo cubes.

Having a vegetable-growing allotment provided by one's local authority was much appreciated. An island nation, Britain was far from self-sufficient. For this reason, everyone was encouraged to grow their own food, to make do, and to mend everything rather than replace. Many women became dressmakers while men unfit or too old for service learned to be self-reliant, to become their own cobblers, tailors and gardeners.

The allotment allocated to our family was situated in the grounds of the Catholic church opposite our home. After the outbreak of war, this ground had been divided into small squares or plots of land. Each family living in Cheam's larger square, known as Tabor Gardens, had an allotment for their family needs and ours was number 49. Of course, families helped each other and there was much bartering which helped everyone to avoid going short.

The needs of children are quite different from those of adults and perish the thought that children could survive without their sweets. With our pocket money, we purchased our weekly ration of Crunchie Bars and Mars Bars.

Other favourites included Callard and Bowser toffees and Butterscotch sweets and chocolate. As innovative as ever, Mother was inspired to use a large empty biscuit tin as a savings bank for our sweets. Having purchased as much confectionary as the family ration books would allow, the candies would be banked and withdrawn on special occasions. At the end of, say, a two-week period of restraint, we would enjoy a great feast. As we grew older, we had midnight feasts too, and these naturally were well attended.

Each morning the allowance of milk was delivered to the doorsteps of Cheam's population. The different-coloured tops were gold, silver or metallic depending upon the cream content of the milk in each bottle. Unfortunately for most families, the tit family of birds quickly learned that a stabbing beak could easily pierce a milk bottle's metallic top. The offending winged scoundrel would then use its bill as a straw to fill its tummy at our expense. The marauders even learned that the gold tops promised a creamier content than did the silver tops. It was a matter of speculation as to how garden birds could distinguish the difference in milk quality from the colour of the bottle tops. At least they are not colour blind.

Necessity being the mother of invention, Dad had the solution and, fashioning a small wooden board to cover the bottle tops, suggested to the milkman that he use it each time he delivered our milk. It worked okay.

Deliveries by horse and cart had the added advantage of also delivering a trail of horse manure. There was a great rivalry as to which of the neighbours could fastest emerge from their homes with shovel and bucket. Collecting horse manure provided additional pocket money for boys prepared to beat the adults to these equine deposits. If dung were dropped in front of a home, it was considered the householder's privilege to own the deposit. Woe to neighbours who disregarded this unwritten community rule. Each deposit of horse manure was considered a personal possession and was used in the allotments and gardens.

We were situated close to London, so the air raids by the Luftwaffe became a regular fact of life as World War II progressed. We were all on the frontlines during that dark period of Britain's history. Upon hearing the sirens, Mother would quickly gather me up in her arms or take me by my hand rushing to the under-stairs closet. There, she would place me down on the floor in the foetal position before lying on top of me to shield me with her body.

There was a nearby air-raid shelter that could be used. If sufficient warning allowed, we would quickly gather blankets and any small comforts that we could place in a bag. These useful items would include a thermos flask, after which we would make our way to the shelter as quickly as possible.

Subsequent to the Allied invasion of France in June 1944, the Germans started to use V-1 flying bombs to target London. Nicknamed Doodlebugs, the missiles were so named because we could hear them coming. The V-1s could either drop to a given target or they could glide on wings until the flying missile reached its target. In either case, one prepared for the strike after each flying bomb's engine became silent. The frightening silence that followed was afterwards followed by an explosion as these weapons detonated on impact.

For us, it was a bit like listening to a thunderstorm and calculating the time between the lightning flash and the thunderclap, which would suggest how close the impact would be. Our fears about becoming a victim were not unfounded. Several homes near to our home were struck. One Doodlebug actually landed in our garden but failed to explode.

Shortly after this awful experience, my mother decided we two should move to her sister's house in Derby. London and southern England were increasingly being targeted by the Luftwaffe. I was now nearly four years of age, so it was time for my name being added to the Derby school's register of pupils, where I was to be a pupil for almost one year. Of course, my recollections are vague. However, I do recall that I had a natural rapport with my bicycle, and I peddled each day to my school and back. It was a scary time for children for above our heads barrage balloons hovered. In fact, these aerial balloons protected us as the wire cables strewing from each balloon deterred invading aircraft. I recall constantly hiding under the table to avoid becoming a victim of bombs and not understanding I was afraid of the balloons!

As the war drew to a close it was thought safe enough for us to return to our home in Cheam. Again, there was just my mother and I at home. My father, a British Army captain, was constantly away and stationed in Northern Ireland.

When on several occasions he visited us there was much excitement. We delighted in his very smart army uniform, particularly the buttons; as the saying goes, 'as bright as a soldier's button'! My father used to polish his uniform buttons with a gadget designed for the purpose. Father cleaning his buttons was a task that fascinated me. I have never forgotten my feeling of great pride when on occasion I was allowed the privilege of using the polishing liquid to bring his buttons up to the gleaming standard expected of the officer class.

Other than my ability as a cyclist, I was drawn to dancing, an interest which became the love of my life. How carefully I examined my amateurish performances when I practised in front of the full-length mirror that was a feature of our lounge. Mindful of giving her only child the lead and inspiration she needed, my mother enrolled me in a course of ballet lessons at a local dancing school.

Attendance of my first public performances was exclusively the privilege of my father when he was home on service leave. Alas, as the lessons were conducted exclusively in the French language, an idiom I found difficult to master, there was little choice but to quit my lessons. However, my love for dancing never left me.

CHAPTER THREE
MY SCHOOLING

IT WAS usual for young children to be enrolled in a school considered most appropriate to their locality. Being a very normal child, and fitting in well with my peers, I was entered on the register of Sutton High School. This was our term for the school that was more formally known as the Girls Public Day School Trust (GPDST). Our school competed with nearby schools, e.g., Putney and Streatham Schools in sports.

Ahead of me lay nine years of happy schooling and, as a bonus, it was located just a mile away from our home. We pupils walked or cycled to school each day regardless of the weather. For certain I was a blithe spirit in my school uniform as I peddled along the country lanes. During my daily trips to and from school, I found my mind would peddle as fast as my tiny legs.

Fitting in well with the school's environment the little Jill (Curzon) was described by her teachers as an "all-rounder". Being a sporty person with a competitive streak, I excelled at netball, hockey, and yes, I was in our first eleven Cricket team. I loved tennis and fondly recall my parent's pride when at Junior Wimbledon I reached the third round. I was also a member of the school's diving team, and perhaps I had been a fish in an earlier life, as I don't recall being intimidated by the height of the swimming pool's diving board. My performance in the more academic subjects was equally strong, hence my being dubbed an all-rounder.

Was I trying to please myself, my family or my friends, or was I simply following the dots and turning chance to opportunity whenever I could?

Looking back, I was a reserved child and unassuming by nature. That might simply be an English characteristic that I had adapted to. My close friends were few in number and this suited the loner in me.

I am certain much credit goes to our schoolteachers for my contentment and success during my school years. Our tutors at Sutton High were committed and were enthusiastic about both their subjects and the well-being of their pupils. Much credit must also go to my having a very good memory. Such recall was useful when during History lessons I remembered dates long enough to pass exams, but this facility was not strong enough to keep in my otherwise busy little head.

It must be remembered too that my parents were very well educated. Like many mothers of the make-do period, Mum had a diverse set of skills. Being a trained tailor, she was also a competent dressmaker, making all my clothes including my school uniforms, my navy tunics and white Viyella blouses, and summer dresses of mauve and white checked cotton. If anything was a challenge too far then, she adapted, modified, repaired and in many cases improved. I often ask myself where on earth Mother found the time to qualify as a chemist while at the same time mastering the intricacies of playing the melodic pianoforte. My mother taught me so many things and different skills that have helped me all my life.

From 1945 onward the shortcomings and sacrifices of war became little more than a memory. Rationing came to an end and from midnight of July 4th, 1954, meaning we could finally dispense with those horrid ration books. About to be opened was an Aladdin's cave stuffed with foods and fruits of a kind we had never dreamed about, let alone imagined we would one day have.

As I approached the end of my education, my day-to-day language adapted, and there were new terms to be considered, such as 'the opposite sex'. My goodness, look around, there are boys out there too. Still, such thoughts were purely platonic, for the habits of yesterday were far different than they are today.

We were excited by our impending school skiing trip to Austria, combined with a similar invitation going to a boys' school. During our stay in Austria, the boys were accommodated in Lech while the girls stayed at The Sonnenburg Hotel in the village of Oberlech, situated a little higher up the mountain and not too distant from Salzburg.

We thoroughly enjoyed ten days amidst breathtaking mountain scenery set against a backdrop of clear blue sky. However, calamity beckoned during our first lesson in skiing. While standing still listening to the instructor on perfectly level ground, I somehow lost my balance and fell forward flat on my face. During the upset, my skis somehow crossed in the air behind me, and my right knee was badly twisted. Not so much as take a bow as take a fall, Jill!

The outcome was that I spent the next eight days on the hotel terrace with my leg bandaged, reading and listening to music, which was echoing round the surrounding hills like *The Sound of Music*. Meanwhile everyone else had a wonderful time on the slopes. Then, as fast as the bandages came off, the weather deteriorated. We soon experienced at first-hand the fury of a snow blizzard.

Never say die unless you mean to do so. I defied instruction and common-sense. Naughtily, I conspired with my friend Janet to go off on our own. It would give my chum opportunity to practice her newly learned skills and me an opportunity to begin again where I had finished off. My reason for doing so was the desire to tell everyone at home that I had been skiing in Austria, but I stretched both my ligaments and the truth.

Boy meets girl and, for some, the outcomes fall short of vows solemnly made at the altar. Despite my disability, I went to a dance attended by the students of both the boys and the girls' schools. To make certain there would be no drifting from the shining path the occasion was closely supervised, and we were all back at our hotels at 10pm.

Janet met her future husband at this event and the two stayed happily married. I, meanwhile, brought home with me the love of garlic, with which I had become acquainted. It was a love affair that was shared with my lifelong love of Wiener schnitzel.

Was there another great love waiting for me lurking behind the theatre curtains?

Back home, the two schools joined forces in staging the end of term plays with a preference for Gilbert and Sullivan productions. The favourite operettas were *Iolanthe* and *The Gondoliers* and both were performed by students at the public hall in Sutton. From lipstick to slapstick and greasepaint all was now set to encourage my playing prominent roles in movie and television productions.

Ours was very much a conventional middle-class life. As I progressed through my teenage years, I became a member of Cheam's two tennis clubs, while each week's educational and social rituals were crowned by Sunday services held at the town's church. Our teenage years were a kaleidoscope of incidents, experiences, and coffee bar trivia rather than drama. Ours was a life of security that provided the perfect starting point for life.

In the 1950s, Bill Haley & His Comets burst on to the world of rock and roll music. Ours was an optimistic age as the world danced in the aisles to 'Rock Around the Clock', 'See You Later Alligator', 'Shake, Rattle and Roll' and 'Skinny Minny'. The effect of rock and roll on the staid post-war generation was a revolution in music and much else besides.

Where else to go on a Saturday evening but the village

hop, where we jived until we dropped. I thought the ideal skirt to be a mid-calf length skirt made from a completely circular, flat piece of material. The pleasing result converted into a pirouetting circle when one spun round. Purchasing the appropriate sizes in royal blue and black taffeta the skirt was soon ready. Using mother's Singer Sewing Machine, I made my new skirt in a single afternoon at the end of which I cried out '*Voilà!*' The skirt was reversible, being blue one side and black the other. That evening was a huge success. My only regret was that over time my skirt and I went our separate ways.

While enjoying tennis I made many new friends and one was a boy named John Boryer. My new pal was the son of some of my parents' close friends. In fact, John's mother had once been engaged to my mother's brother. Yes, ours was a small and socially cloistered world. Everybody knew everyone else and identified with their family history and knowledge of their working and social lives.

CHAPTER FOUR
THE TEENAGER

THE OTHER meeting place was the church. Each Sunday evening, I went to Cheam's St Dunstan's Presbyterian Church of England. We teenagers always sat in the back pews and giggled rather a lot, I'm afraid. The sombre seriousness of the service was shattered whenever one of us would accidentally drop a coin or would giggle. Then it would escalate and pretty soon everyone was giggling, and we were scolded at times. After church, the kids met outside and, after chatting, would go off to the village coffee bar. This rendezvous was modern and popular with the teenagers, and I was first introduced to frothy coffee. At no time in my life was tea a drink to pass my lips. While happy enough to make tea for friends and visitors I was unlikely to join them; I just did not like the smell of it, which was so un-English of me.

My boyfriend John was always with me when we were going to dances, or hops as they were otherwise known. John had his friends too, but unlike many he didn't attend the Country Grammar School. My friend went instead to a private school known as Downsend School situated near Leatherhead. Both John's parents and mine were also good friends and they were very much part of our social activities.

At that time, one could safely say that John and I were

dating and were considered a couple. Our togetherness took us rambling through the local park, on shopping excursions, or socialising and learning about life through our visits to local farms, where we enjoyed the playfulness of the new-born lambs. To top it all there was the wandering gypsy fair that arrived each summer and which added colour and gaiety to our local park.

Another much-loved interest was ice skating. Every Saturday morning, accompanied by friends, we would breathlessly catch the train to Streatham Ice Rink. Often there was a girl at the rink who I imagined to be about eighteen years of age. Enchanted by her panache I watched as she effortlessly glided and pirouetted. I dreamed that one day my ability to skate on ice would also match hers. When I later met Roger Moore, he told me that he too skated there on Saturday mornings.

Each Friday afternoon I would go with Vivien, another school friend. Accompanied by her mother, my friend was taking lessons in figure skating at Richmond Ice Rink. I was more interested in freestyle than figure skating and I was tutored in ice waltz, foxtrot, and quickstep and such dance routines. Becoming quite focused on this new interest, I was to enjoy skating for several years.

A number of years later I again met the girl who had so enthralled and inspired me when I first took an interest in ice skating. In the intervening years, she had become an actress, and we met in Gerry's, an actors' club, and became quite good friends. It was so nice to have an opportunity to tell her how much I had admired and respected her when as a teen I had taken up ice skating.

John and I were very much an item. In love with each other, we spent hours planning our lives together. Then, as happens, there was the night when our canoodling went a little too far. The outcome of overstepping the mark was the realisation that, at just sixteen, I was pregnant. Now what? It was 1954, when the convention was much stricter than it is today. And, still at school I was preparing to take my all-important life-changing GCSE examinations.

There's never a good time to become pregnant out of wedlock. Finding out I was 'preggers' was definitely a massive zero in my life, and of course, it would be shocking news for my parents too.

John and I desperately tried to figure out a solution to the predicament. My parents at this point were blissfully unaware of my condition and my distress. Catching a train to London I contacted The Good Samaritans, managed by Chad Varah.

Frightened out of my wits I found myself wandering in a haze in which there simply didn't seem to be an exit. I was distraught, inconsolable and felt very much isolated from the world around me. Although praying to God was hardly new to me, I recall constantly doing so during these difficult days. I recall Chad Varah understood, and as he comforted me he gave me the best possible advice.

For me, it was a great relief to have someone non-judgemental to talk through my dilemmas with. John, in the meantime, was doing his best to find out about the possibility of abortion but was not meeting with success. Realising that we were far too young for marriage, which would be opposed by our families anyway, we two lovers were truly caught up in a no-win situation.

Finally, there was no alternative but to come clean with my parents, as Chad Varah had said. To my undying gratitude, I recall their taking the news calmly and without the terrible scolding and humiliation I had anticipated. I am under no illusions as to how deeply the news wounded my mother and, it must be said, my father too. Father, being the archetypical English army officer, was thoughtful and kept a stiff upper lip. I felt that I had let both of them down and a sense of deep shame was added to my pathos.

With calmness, my parents took over from that point on and this lessened the weight on my overburdened shoulders. It was against this comforting backdrop that my schooling continued. Because of my petite size, I was not showing my condition, and I maintained sufficient composure to pass eight O Levels. Constantly driven by the need for me to make amends I worked hard to show my parents how appreciative I was of their understanding and support.

This is where family can show their true colours. My mother's brother was a heart and lung surgeon in a Harley Street practice. On an earlier occasion, my uncle had performed an operation on the gall bladder of the matron at Southend General Hospital. The operation had been a success and, appreciative of his skills, the kindly matron agreed to take me under her wing upon her hearing of my plight. Gratefully, this wayward teen packed her bags and caught the train so that I might stay with the matron as her guest until my child was born.

As I had already passed my Preliminary Nursing Exam at school it was an easy matter to employ me as a cadet nurse in her hospital. Nursing became my occupation until December 1955, at which point such work was proving far too difficult for me. Life was made easier due to the matron being a genuinely lovely and caring woman. She enjoyed my company and, of course, I made myself useful around her home and this taught me new domestic skills.

My matron mentor loved playing the piano and was sufficiently talented to paint and make her own Christmas cards. The matron had never married and, through our companionship, I learned a great deal about human kindness while picking up new skills. We two bonded and we became firm friends and remained so. I pause to think that this experience teaches us that every cloud has a silver lining.

As the saying in the nursing profession goes, all was as well as could be expected. My newborn child arrived one week late but the birth was perfectly normal despite the fact that I was only just seventeen. My baby girl Pamela was immediately taken away without there being a chance for us to bond. As was standard practice in such circumstances my breasts were bound. I was given medicine so the naturally produced mother's milk wouldn't be produced.

My uncle, the Harley Street surgeon, had arranged for my child to be adopted. Sadly, I never saw or heard anything of her from the moment of birth, when she left my sight. I did have a photo of my child taken when she was twelve years old. The occasion was a music event in Westcliff, near Southend-on-Sea in the south east of England. Her name now was Stefanie and her photograph was a consequence of a thoughtful gesture by my matron friend, who had sent the picture to me. The much-loved snap stayed with me and in my wallet for years afterwards.

Upon returning to my family home in Cheam I learned that in the meantime heads had been put together and my parents had plans for me. Unaware of the real reason for my absence the neighbourhood welcomed my return. Having a child outside of marriage was still something of a scandal to be gossiped about. But those who live in glass houses should not throw stones. All communities have their fair and unfair share of skeletons in their cupboards. I am sure mine was an innocent fall from grace when compared to some.

I had been spoken well of as a cadet nurse, but I realised that this career was not for Jill Curzon. Being of a sensitive nature I couldn't bear to see people suffer in pain and discomfort and nor was I enamoured of the sight of blood. The medical profession calls for carers of compassion, empathy and detachment, love without attachment; I failed to qualify in each vital part.

My pragmatic mother, constantly mindful of the importance of acquiring new skills, introduced me to St. James's Secretarial College in London. There I would receive a good basic education that would stand me in good stead in whatever I wanted to do in the future. Yet, always at the back of my mind was my desire to be an actress and my parents were aware of my yearning.

The marriage option was never an issue with John's parents or mine and were two were not to see each other again. This was not easy for me as he was the only person I could empathise with.

CHAPTER FIVE
LIFE AND LOVE AS A SECRETARY

THERE WAS nothing to do but live with reality rather than dreams of what might have been yet could never be. I enjoyed life at St. James's Secretarial College in London. I had barely settled in when I made a very good friend, whose friendship would sustain me throughout my life. Close friends we were, but I couldn't bring myself to share my secret with her. I don't think this was anything to do with the fear of disapproval but rather my need to accept my past in secret silence.

Inseparable, Anne and I enjoyed our lunches at Joe Lyons' restaurant located by South Kensington Station. Each day, we travelled to town from our homes, Anne from Woking and me from my home in Cheam. Dad also travelled to London every day, but to London Bridge, where he worked in the city for the Union Discount Company.

Anne's dad worked in the perfumery profession. He taught Anne about essences and how to identify them. My good friend developed quite a good nose. At the end of the secretarial courses, we were congratulated and received diplomas in shorthand typing and in bookkeeping. My friend excelled at speed typing while I passed shorthand writing with colours flying.

With immediate effect, we were sent for interviews around London as there was a demand for trained secretaries. My first job was at Hammersmith Hospital, working in the clinical secretariat pool as they called it. The hospital provided for eighty doctors, requiring the support of ten secretaries. This meant of course that we secretaries provided for the needs of eight doctors each.

Ours was a heavy workload and required an aptitude for if not experience in medical jargon. We newcomers were thrown in at the deep end and expected to get on with it. Bear in mind also that the maxim is true: the handwriting of doctors leaves much to be desired, still today! It didn't get any better, as doctors also have a habit of abbreviating everything they write. This caused further confusion as we secretaries were daily dealing with medical terms and pharmaceutical products we were wholly unfamiliar with.

The advice was to acquire a medical dictionary, but even so the job was beyond my abilities and I lasted just the week. Anne also had her share of new job challenges but in the end landed a job as a trainee secretary for Elizabeth Arden cosmetics. Anne loved the job and the job loved her. Her appointment provided her with a great career for years to come.

Still a teenager, but turning nineteen in 1957 so only just, I found a new position at Coleman, Prentis and Varley, one of the top six advertising companies in London. The agency's offices were situated at 34 Grosvenor Street in Mayfair. Now I too was a round peg in a round hole just like my friend, taking to advertising and marketing like a duck takes to water. There was the added bonus of being assigned to a small group to which in turn had been allocated a number of quality clients. Our clients included Shell and our office found the inspiration and teamwork needed to create the Bulldog Campaign that attracted national recognition.

Another of our team's clients was McVitie's Digestive

Biscuits. A bonus was that we had lots of samples of these wonderful, yummy biscuits coated with milk chocolate to be enjoyed with our morning coffee. Yet another client was the Territorial Army, who had in mind a recruitment campaign.

None of the firm's executives in the group headed by Peter Long wanted to be bothered with that one. For this reason, I was promoted to account executive to take charge of the Territorial Army account. The advertising prerequisite was primarily focused on Britain's Territorial Army recruitment. Despite its title, the TA is an army made up of part-time soldiers. Unless on training or called up in an emergency the service personnel keep their civilian jobs.

I was selected to work with the British Army's top brass. To be fair, the high-ranking officers were courteous towards me, although they were taken aback at a macho role being discussed with such a sweet young thing as I appeared to be over the telephone. I enjoyed the challenge but wasn't surprised at the lack of enthusiasm for the job displayed by my colleagues. I supposed my having an army officer father helped me to understand their requirements.

During that year at Coleman, Prentis and Varley we completed several contracts for the firm's International Division, located a short walk away in Park Lane. There, Derek Partridge was delegated to interact with our office; he was in the department because he was conversant with seven languages. There was chemistry between us and occasional lunches together were soon part of our routine. One of our favourite eateries was the Sandwich Shop in Mount Street. If the weather was convivial, we would take our lunches to the park.

As we got to know each other better I must admit that I was very much smitten. My amiable and handsome companion was half-English and half-American. His mother was from Baltimore and his father was typically British – in fact, a major in the army who was later assigned to MI5.

Derek's father was one of the initiators and founders of the Palestine Police Force. He was also an excellent cricketer and the wicket keeper for the local team in Limpsfield, near Oxted in Surrey, where they lived. In those days there was not much protection for wicket keepers. Frederick, my beau's father, unfortunately, received more than his fair share of blows to the head. The blows caused him to develop the brain tumour that eventually killed him. Derek's mother, Louise, was quite artistic and a creative homemaker involved in many local projects. She was a great gardener and was invariably surrounded by her pet dachshunds. Derek and his mother lived in a beautiful old Queen Anne house called "The Bower" that she later converted into two well-appointed apartments.

Happy in my role as an advertising secretary I travelled up to Victoria from Cheam each day to work at Coleman, Prentis and Varley. Derek took the train from Oxted to Victoria to his job at the firm's other department. As often as our schedules allowed, we met for lunch and then each evening we travelled to our respective homes.

We were now very much in love and my parents invited Derek to take tea with us at our family home. I think he enjoyed the experience and I, in turn, was invited to meet his parents. The outcome was that our parents approved of our relationship and many pleasant weekends were spent together at The Bower in Limpsfield. Derek and I had much in common. Idealistic and young, we believed that the world we lived in was a much better place than in reality it was. Blissfully naïve, I suppose we both had much to learn about the world.

They were optimistic times as World War II was fast becoming a distant and fading memory. There was much for young people to be optimistic about and Derek and I were no exception. On the crest of a growing wave of optimism and innovation, social change and growing prosperity brought opportunities to take advantage of. Ours was a brave new world; it was a time of renaissance, creativity and fun accompanied by cheerfulness and joy. Everyone was bursting with energy and no one had time for negativity or cynicism.

It was also a rebellious age in which the social mores of yesterday were increasingly challenged and replaced with newfound freedom. There was new opportunity for rebellious voices to be raised and heard. As we entered the swinging sixties we welcomed this new age, as our liberated generation had the past and the present with which to make comparisons.

I am unsure if we realised it at the time, but looking back to 1958, surely we could not have timed our entry into the world better. There was simply no better time to be a twenty-year-old than in the swinging sixties.

Derek and I became firmly attached. Our ideals and aspirations combined with our innocence and similar backgrounds assured us that our future was made in heaven. In all respects we were compatible. We chatted endlessly, inspiring each other as we talked through this and that.

The weekends we spent together flew by, each filled with domestic conviviality. Derek's mum was a splendid cook and, having experienced service during the war, my boyfriend's father was the perfect conversationalist. As we drifted off to sleep in our respective beds we shared a resignation that another week at work would slowly pass before we were together as a family again.

CHAPTER SIX
FIRST MARRIAGE

IT WAS inevitable that marriage would follow and, without a doubt, both our parents had now assumed our betrothal. Seemingly, fate was in full agreement, and on February 8th, 1958, a cool blustery late winter's day, we two tied the knot at Epsom registrar's office. Our nuptials completed, we gathered our wits together for the wonderful reception that had been arranged for us.

This celebration of our wedding was to take place at the historic Nonsuch Park. This residence is one of the loveliest castles imaginable and it is set in huge grounds then a public park in Cheam. What fun we had; my family of guests was very large and it had been arranged that a Beefeater in full regalia would meet and greet us and, in fact, he played the part of the Lord Chamberlain throughout the merriment that followed.

For a bride, there was no better setting, especially the right royal occasion being celebrated at a castle. On that day I was an absolute princess, and being the focus of attention, I received endless compliments. Our parents beamed with joy and satisfaction as well they might. My recollections are of the loveliest event imaginable. Especially noteworthy was my outfit including a hat that I had myself made for the occasion the night before.

Derek's all-consuming hobby was rough shooting using a twelve-bore shotgun. Because of his passion we were never going to be short of game for the table, which included game birds, rabbits and hares. A similar enthusiasm was for clay pigeon shooting. It, therefore, seemed perfectly natural to spend our honeymoon with a farmer friend whose home and grounds were located in Lincolnshire. It was the perfect location for early morning duck shooting, and in the evening we would turn our attention and our shotgun barrels on the wood pigeons as they flew home to roost.

It must be said that my interest in shooting had been entirely inspired by Derek's passion. Thanks to him I soon became skilled with a game gun, most importantly learning the safe use of guns and ammunition. What went in stayed in. All these years later I still cringe if I see such a gun being handled inappropriately.

So, we recently betrothed were in the Lincolnshire countryside in the middle of February. One might suppose that such a bleak farm in sub-zero temperatures, sleeping in an unheated farmhouse, as being no one's idea of the perfect honeymoon! To add a little spice, we were aroused from our bed in the very early hours each morning. Suitably attired we would troop off in the pre-dawn darkness to a hunter's primitive hide in the Lincolnshire marshlands to wait for the ducks to show themselves.

The evenings were easier and more productive and typically we would bag thirty to forty pigeons and, after bagging the birds, take them to the train station in our Morris Minor. The game's eventual destination was our butcher's display cabinets back in Limpsfield village in Surrey. The other side of the coin was our being paid for the game, which more or less paid for our honeymoon. However, the high spot for me was to return home with a recipe for a yummy sponge cake that we often enjoyed.

It occurred to me that there was more to marriage than romance.

Our first home was a rented cottage situated on a farmer's property in Westerham in the Kent countryside that was well placed for our daily commute to London. Over time, Derek lost interest in marketing and advertising and was became attracted to the stock market, which at the time was booming.

This was a pivotal part of our lives because separately I was drawn to the acting profession, which pleasingly involved dancing routines. Enraptured by the thought of my taking part in stage performances I spent hours of solitude dancing in an interpretive way. I practised to a wide selection of music genre that ranged from pop to Latin American, jazz and soul.

Derek quit his job after being successful in his stock market interests and we made plans for our future. It was about this time that the rapport between us was unravelling. Realising something was amiss we had a heart to heart in which he confessed that he longed to be a free spirit in an open marriage. Of course, we would remain good friends but not exclusively so.

Derek had this air-fairy notion of our being committed to an abiding friendship and companionship for the rest of our lives. There would be other ladies in his life too, so basically my husband wanted his cake while eating it. Oh yes, and he added that he had no wish to father children!

I was totally devastated by the conversation as I had been looking forward to keeping our wedding vows, working things through together, and raising our own family. Earlier on in our relationship, I had told him about Stefanie and he was both understanding and supportive. However, I couldn't but wonder why he had not disclosed this yearning to be a free spirit before we were married.

Looking back on events I assume he thought that our rapport would entice me into his free spirit way of life.

Oh boy, I thought to myself. *What a mess.*

The atmosphere between us didn't improve, when to add salt to the wound he said with a smile, 'Well, what's good for the gander is good for the goose too.'

The implication was that I was free to do as I wished and I was at liberty to make inappropriate friendships. Our conversation took my breath away. I was appalled at his directness and his audacity to make such a presumption. Nothing could have been further from my mind.

Being in love with Derek I couldn't come to terms with his cavalier approach to our marriage and the vows we had so solemnly made. Realising I was talking to a man quite different from the fiancé I had married I began to withdraw into myself. In such circumstances acceptance and the gathering of one's thoughts don't happen overnight; one needs time and space to come to terms with the change in one's circumstances.

With the passage of time, I had little choice but to realise that what had happened was no aberration; I was seeing another side to Derek that he had so far kept concealed. When acceptance finally brought some kind of closure our lives outwardly appeared to be as routine as before. On the other hand, it was clear that Derek was not going to change and I was never going to accept marriage on his terms. It was time to accept that this was the beginning of the end of our marriage.

One nice thing to remember was a lovely break Derek's parents gave us near to Christmas 1961, when they invited us to go with them on a cruise to the Canary Islands. It was on a Greek liner called the *Lakonia*. It was a very pleasant trip, especially the visit to Maderia and the famous Reid's Hotel on the cliff top. We did occasionally wonder at how old the ship was; when we had a fire drill, the bollards around which the ropes for lowering the lifeboats were bound were covered in so many layers of white paint they would never have moved in an emergency. After our trip the ship was taking to Southampton to repair the sprinkler system, and right after that, the very next voyage in fact, the ship caught fire and it was a terrible disaster. It sank, and about one hundred and twenty-eight people died, the bodies of fifty-five people buried in Gibraltar. I guess we were very lucky to have avoided that!

CHAPTER SEVEN
JEFF WILCOX

USING THE money from his stock market pursuits, Derek purchased a cottage called Riverside situated by the river in Penshurst, Kent. One day, a young man whose motorcycle had broken down knocked on our door to ask if we could offer assistance. The ever-obliging Derek invited him in and, as the two hit it off immediately, he was to stay as Derek's guest for two days.

Jeff Wilcox was working for Massey Ferguson and told us he lived near Croydon in Surrey. Derek and our unexpected visitor became wrapped up in each other and, at some point, there was talk of them partnering a business. This was to lead to their registering a company that was to be known as Mechanical Gardening. Derek took care of most of the investment and he set about ordering the company's stationery and arranging the management of the business.

The plan was that Jeff Wilcox would canvass owners of homes that were clearly burdened by an overgrown garden in dire need of professional maintenance. Having estimated what was needed to restore the garden, a price would be offered and, upon acceptance, Derek made sure that Jeff had everything needed to carry out the work and worked alongside him. I, meanwhile, provided the refreshments.

Of special interest were homes that were untidy due to their owners' absence or because they were on the market. The effect of the two men's labours was very pleasing. It was obvious that their enterprise was destined for success.

During his doorstep encounters Jeff was greeted by a French lady whose husband was the head of Bata shoes. She was the mother of two children and it transpired that her marriage was in difficulties. The outcome was that after meeting Jeff she sued for divorce, after which she and Jeff married.

Derek was becoming bored with the tedium and lack of challenge and handed the business over to his partner to enable him to make a fresh and independent start. Jeff opened a garden nursery in the countryside and made a great success of it. Before long he was importing stock from abroad, including thousands of tulips from Amsterdam, during which time his business expanded as did the payroll. The market garden business proved to be profitable and enabled Jeff and Claudine to purchase a country estate. As one might expect, the estate's gardens were testimony to their hard work and skill. All that was necessary for them to complete their lives was a pair of dachshund dogs.

Their life seemed to be bliss... But was it? With the passing of years, I picked up hearsay that suggested that Jeff was drinking very heavily. As alcoholism ran its course, he became the dearly departed. Going off the rails altogether, the once successful entrepreneur was caught up in some rebellious movement based in London, and over time became belligerent and confrontational. This change in his nature led to him being arrested and apparently the saga came to a sad end. Claudine had little choice but to accept the end of their relationship and sold up. I heard afterwards that she had moved to Menorca and led a quiet contented life.

Derek was still profiting from his stock market interests and we lived comfortably, decorating the cottage ourselves. We were wrapped up in our dream of turning a cottage into a home that reflected our tastes. After each week's hard work, we ate easily prepared chicken dinners which had been put in the deepfreeze.

The curtains I made from material I had chosen matched the colours of each of the cottage's rooms splendidly. As there were parquet floors in the main living room and terracotta tiles in the hall, a scattering of kitchen rugs complemented our décor perfectly.

Ours was now everyone's idea of a dream cottage but sadly our lives were not quite as dreamlike. On the upside, my other dream pursuit was still at the forefront of my mind.

CHAPTER EIGHT
A CAREER AS A THESPIAN AND A CLAY PIGEON SHOOTER

I SOON realised that Derek needed change and challenge in his life too. My husband had initially been drawn into advertising agency work after his being chosen as having the perfect image to reflect the army's idea of the impeccable poster soldier. The army at the time of Derek's engagement was working on a national recruitment drive. I think that seeing himself as a model inspired Derek, for he liked soaking up the attention.

Separately, I was chosen to be a model in the Amplex advertisements. The company's remedy for bad breath was featured in their adverts displaying an attractive woman flanked by male and female companions looking askance at her, her breath clearly leaving something to be desired. As one can well imagine, the agency found difficulty in recruiting a female model for such a photoshoot. Made of sterner stuff I volunteered for the shoot, and soon afterwards London's double-decker buses and the city's underground railway network were festooned with images of Jill whose breath was mindful of an unwashed armpit. At least the campaign didn't reflect negatively on me personally as the girl in the advert was wearing a mask. Such was the inglorious genesis of my career as an actress.

The publicity we gained on behalf of our respective advertising agencies was to open more doors for us. Such a promising start inspired Derek to engage an agent and he subsequently featured in several television commercials. One thing inspires another, so to further improve his career he joined a repertory company to acquire the skills he needed for the acting profession.

My inclination was similar to his, but as most of my peers were by now graduating in the thespian arts it seemed I had left matters too late. In 1962, Derek stepped in and introduced me to a repertory company at Tunbridge Wells, called The Penguin Players. I was given a start and what a start it was I am thankful to say. Filled with excitement and fired by enthusiasm, I began what was to be one of the busiest and most absorbing parts of my life.

Working eighteen-hour days as an assistant stage manager (ASM), which included being the prop girl, I had responsibility for the décor of the theatre production. Despite its small size, my Austin Healey helped enormously as I busied myself borrowing, and by shamelessly cajoling, I acquired the necessary furniture.

In Rep, you rehearse one play during the day and perform another during the evening. Furthermore, as an ASM you have to be what is called "the book", who, out of audience sight, prompts the performers should they forget their lines. If during a performance you are chosen to play the part of a character, delivering one or two lines, then this is a bonus. But otherwise one is the dogsbody, at hand to plaster over the cracks. During the summer we toured and performed in Blackpool, Bristol and Brighton.

There was no possibility of my taking a break, for my life remained as hectic as ever. That year I played a part in about ten television commercials such as the tobacco giants, Woodbines, Rothmans and State Express Cigarettes. The Woodbine commercial was shot on the River Thames while sailing in a small boat, and with the ubiquitous camera crew present, it was great fun.

It was pointed out to me that it wasn't the practice of competing tobacco companies to use the same actors, as viewers would recognise them, but for some reason my working for tobacco giant rivals didn't seem to cause a problem. I guess I looked sufficiently different in each one.

One of my commercials included a promotion by Oxydol that was at the same time an introduction to a top-loading washing machine. The promotion was based on the soap powder company showing how quickly and effectively a Ribena stain could be removed from clothing. The finished blouse was filmed before the stain was added so it was hardly surprising it looked like new after the wash! It was also thought necessary to add a little froth to the washing powder suds and this was done by adding a little dry ice to the water. Who on earth thinks this up?

Most of us are familiar with the book covers of the type used by publishers of romance novels. One of my engagements was with the agency acting on behalf of Pan Books. Here was an opportunity for me to dress up as Nell Gwyn or a Native American tribal beauty. The latter required a model with suitably black hair. I think that occasion was the first time in my life I had sported plaits, and some of the shooting sequences called upon my training as an actress.

My weekends were not spent relaxing, as Derek's enthusiasm for clay pigeon shooting was undiminished. We attended events all over England and Wales.

Derek bought a Bedford Dormobile, which saved on the hotel bills. Our vehicle was mechanically reliable and reasonably comfortable, with a bunk bed on both sides and a mini kitchenette where we were able to wash and do a little cooking. For the other necessities of life, we used caravan and camping sites that had shower and toilet facilities. We didn't always go on overnight trips and often the clay pigeon shooting events were within a few hours' drive of our home.

We were, I suppose, what is now known as celebrities, so the media took a great deal of interest in us. Why not, we were naturals in front of the cameras and we were well-versed in the arts of TV presenters and journalists. Much of the media's interest in me was on account of there being very few ladies involved in clay pigeon shooting. The prizes were many, cups and other pleasing awards and events. Competitions were not exclusively men's but there were very few lady's contestants. We went often to the internationally recognised Bisley shooting grounds. The occasions held a special significance for me. My father, who was an excellent rifle shot, had taken second place in the Queen's Prize at the same shooting grounds when in the British Army.

Another of our events was based at Sealand. This is situated near the Welsh and English border, just a bus ride from the ancient Roman city of Chester. This event took place on the large Jones Balers farmlands and was managed mostly by the Jones brothers, Neil and Allan. This was where we met the Formula 1 racing ace Jackie Stewart for the first time, many years before his racing career started. He had travelled down from Dumbarton. The ace driver was very good at clay pigeon shooting and only by a narrow margin did he miss being chosen for the Olympics.

On another occasion, my husband and I took our Dormobile to Paris, where we parked up in the Bois de Boulogne, where they were holding La Coupe des Nations. This is an international Clay Pigeon Shooting Association (CPSA) event using the Olympic Trench layout. The clays travel at an impressive 90 mph instead of the more conventional 60 mph at Down-the-Line shooting events. Also, at each of the event's stands, there is the possibility of three angles and heights from which the clay projectile is launched. This makes the event extremely demanding.

Being a three-day event offered the opportunity for a

splendid French lunch each day. How lovely it was to meet and chat with so many well-heeled influential French people. Here too they shot live pigeons as they were released from traps situated in an adjacent building. By this time, this particular sport had been outlawed in Britain, and we never took part in it anyway. It would soon be forbidden in France, but not quite yet. For this reason, it was still the sport for those who were rich and influential.

In the evening, we were joined by associates who knew Paris well and we enjoyed the great city's nightlife. One of the nightspots we visited was the internationally known Lido. I still have the memento given to me there, a small matchbox with a picture of me dancing printed on its cover. Another place visited was the La Tour d'Argent restaurant, overlooking Notre Dame and the Seine. At the latter, I made friends with Claude Terrail, the owner, who was already a close associate of our new friends. Others we became acquainted with included Baron Claude Foussier, the head of Coca Cola in Paris. Yet another was Le Comte de Riocour, a very charming, cultured and distinguished gentleman. Both were accompanied by their wives. It was a great pleasure to share their company during the three-day international event.

This was my first competition in Olympic Trench. It was a formidable challenge as our lady rivals were as keen as French mustard. The outcome was that Joe Wheater, who was our top shooter, scored ninety-four out of one hundred and thus won the competition. We were elated as this meant that the Cup of Nations would be held in Britain the following year.

Hardly out of my teens, I could look back on a memorable year. 'We are mates,' my husband had said and he was confident that, as close friends, our relationship would last longer and be less stressful. Well, I wasn't wearing rose-tinted spectacles and I was under no illusions as to our marriage's longevity. But whatever the marriage was or wasn't, it suited me too as our careers and our shared interest in shooting was taking up much of our time.

By September 1959, my shooting scores had greatly improved and our feet were well under the tables of the Jones family, our friends who owned and managed the North Wales Gun Club. This was where the Cup of Nations was scheduled to be held. Jackie Stewart came away with the Men's Trophy and I walked blithely on my way with the Lady's Trophy.

Our friends were soon to include Jackie's future wife Helen. About the same time, Allan Jones of Jones Bailers met Shan, who would soon be his wife. Both men were keen on sports cars and I was often invited to join them for a spin in the beautiful North Wales and Wirral countryside. It must be said that both these locations are charming in a bucolic sense. Seemingly unchanged by the passing years there are many thatched cottages and pubs to be seen, rolling landscaped hills and woods, with meandering country lanes. However, such charm was developed over the centuries to be in harmony with pastoral serenity in which a cantering horse was not an absurdity. Imagine then unexpectedly meeting a sports cars careering around hedged bends with the occupants holding their breath in case they too encountered an oncoming vehicle.

Jackie was filled with enthusiasm and he wanted to make progress to qualify for the British Olympic team. As he recalled the occasion in his memoirs, just a single poor score scuppered his chances. But, of course, he went on to do great things by winning the Formula 1 World Racing Driver championship three times. None of us was surprised as he had exceptionally quick reflexes and timing combined with essential self-discipline.

CHAPTER NINE
THE SWINGING SIXTIES

1960 AND 1961 were pivotal for us. There was little choice but to move home for practical reasons. Derek had become friendly with John Kennedy, a businessman and agent. He was the entrepreneur who discovered Tommy Steele and he was now managing his singing career. The two friends had become acquainted at The 2i's coffee bar in Old Compton Street in Soho, where Tommy was performing.

John Kennedy owned two apartments situated on the corner of Curzon and Half Moon streets. They were opposite the Mayfair Hotel. He used the lower apartment as accommodation and the one above as his office. The apartment above had been decorated to the best possible taste and the furnishings were lovely. This home, until he moved to a larger place, was Tommy Steele's pad.

It sounds unbelievable given today's property prices but we secured our domestic heaven at just £4 per week rent. How fortunate we were, for the apartment was perfectly located in Mayfair so everything we needed was but a short distance away.

I had used my savings to purchase my iris-blue Austin Healey Sprite in 1959. Even in the 1960s parking was problematic so I 'played the meters', by which I mean, when they were activated each morning, I would feed mine at two-hour intervals until I was ready to go out. In fairness, it was still much cheaper and easier than it is today.

One day I was driving down Piccadilly and I ran out of petrol in the middle of all the traffic. Luckily, I had a two-gallon tank in the boot of the car so I proceeded to refill it. It was very windy, my hair was blowing, my skirt was too short and even the petrol was splashing! Everybody was staring and hooting. It was so embarrassing I shall never forget it.

Having got to know John Kennedy as both landlord and friend, it was an opportunity for Derek and I to meet show business stars. Many were already successful while others were aspiring actors. We became regular visitors at places where the upwardly mobile gravitated. I became friends with Diana Dors. She had a very impressive personality (and body of course; you did not pass her by without noticing her!) Unlike the more buxom Diana, I was ultra-slim and petite. She was a regular at the many parties we attended back then, and she was always witty and charming. She called me 'Pussycat'. Then, I later heard she referred to some other friends as 'Kitty' and 'Tiger', so she clearly must have had a thing about cats. I always enjoyed her company and humour. She didn't take herself too seriously and everybody loved her for this. She lived with her husband in the house next door to John Kennedy in Maidenhead, down to the River Thames. In retrospect, it's sad that scandal overshadowed most of Diana's life, but she was a terrific actress and shone in films like *Yield to the Night*.

One day, in late October 1961, John Kennedy bought boxes of fireworks ahead of Bonfire Night, storing them in the garden. Unfortunately, a week before the big day, some idiot threw a cigarette end into one of the boxes and set off all the fireworks. The house caught fire and the blaze quickly spread, and tragically three people died and a fourth nearly passed away from a heart attack. Diana herself only just escaped being killed after climbing out of one of the bedroom windows to reach safety.

Another acquaintance was Vidal Sassoon, a close friend of John's. He was already something of a hairstyling legend, whose address book included the most fabulous models of the period. He'd first opened his glamorous hair salon in Mayfair in 1954, and his empire quickly started to grow as many friends and contemporaries became regular clients, and sang his praises to the press every time he changed their hair styles for them.

Was there ever a better time and place in history for someone in their early twenties than Mayfair during the 1960s? Certainly, a renaissance in arty culture seemed to be taking place. It seemed everyone, whatever their circumstances, was enjoying the re-birth of society. The cost of living was affordable, even for the young and aspiring. There were nightclubs starting up everywhere, and as fast as they did so, invitations and memberships were taken up. These haunts offered the opportunity to socialise after the pub closing times at 10.30pm. This was especially important for those working in theatre, as traditionally the pubs would be closing just as final curtain calls were being made. Now, rather than quietly going home through sleeping, soulless streets, we could relax in the comfort of a nightclub.

Those worthy of note included The Village off Sloane Street. It was an intimate, friendly restaurant. This venue was owned by Alex Stirling, very much a socialite and very witty. Alex was on first name terms with fellow trendsetters and fashion models and also owned The Pheasantry in Kings Road. The Establishment in Greek Street first opened in October 1961 and was started by Peter Cook and Dudley Moore. It was mainly a jazz club to begin with, but it quickly started to evolve into the epicentre of London's blossoming satire scene. What a wonderful team Peter made with Dudley Moore; I still find myself copying lots of their infamous Dagenham Dialogues. I used to see a lot of them when I lived in Hampstead and, of course, in *Not Only… But Also*. They were good fun and friends. Dud was a very good pianist, seriously talented.

The Establishment had a nice restaurant presenting two dinner shows, with the downstairs room used for jazz performances and dancing.

Then there was WIPS Club in Leicester Square and the AD-LIB Club situated in Charles's House, Leicester Square. The latter was my favourite. There I could dance until the small hours and not feel too fatigued the following day. Some credit must go to my alcohol self-denial as my preference for dancing left me little time for drinking anything other than water.

Furthermore, dancing kept me fit, not that such was uppermost in my mind, my already lithesome body carrying little excess weight.

There was no stopping the social revolution prevalent in the early sixties. Soon afterwards, the New Arts Club in Great Newport Street opened. By then there was also the well-known Gerry's Actors' Club, situated beneath a ladies' underwear retailer in Shaftesbury Avenue. It was a basement bar restaurant started by Gerald Campion of *Billy Bunter* fame. Another club fondly remembered was the wonderful Buckstone Club found in a Suffolk Street basement.

As an actress, these clubs were very much to my taste and needs. At these watering holes, one would most likely meet professional friends. We would enjoy each other's company and be inspired by personal accounts of success. An added advantage was that the splendid meals, even with trimmings, cost just 12/6, well suited to an actor's measly income.

Popular in the world of advertising agencies and their corporate clients, I was kept busy playing parts in commercials. Looking back, the world of commercial advertising was very innovative. It is interesting that both the pop music and the advertising of the period still resonate decades later. One can still recite the advertising jingles: 'Murray Mint, Murray Mint, too good to hurry mint', 'Persil Washes Whiter', 'You'll wonder where the yellow went when you brush your teeth with Pepsodent'. That's how you know the advertising revival was keeping abreast of the pop world of the time.

During these exciting days, I featured in many commercials on behalf of household name corporations. I was very much part of the passion for good advertising, although, as earlier conceded, some clips were not as honest as they should have been. By this time my portfolio and curriculum vitae were now quite impressive. My past jobs had included Woodbines, Rothmans, Kensitas Cigarettes, the Gallaher Tobacco Group, and State Express.

I was now carrying out assignments for Lifebuoy Soaps, Sifta Salt, Pledge Furniture Polish, Nimble Bread, Glade Polish, Pathé Vintage and Austin Cars. The latter was actually the most charming and evocative documentary. To these might be added Vim and Summer County dairy products. I also modelled for 'Christmas in July' perfume. This fragrance was launched with much fanfare and received accolades from the industry's professionals.

I sometimes wonder if there was a home in the length and breadth of Britain that didn't have a Jill Curzon presence. Books, particularly novels, were as popular as always, while PAN Books was in a class of its own. For these romantic novels, there appeared to be an insatiable appetite. It was such fun to see oneself as a courtesan or a country wench on the covers of these novels. Versatility was the key to my success, and happily for me, my English looks sufficed for different periods of history and indeed varying roles.

At a smidgen over 5' 4", I scored as a model but I was too short in stature for the catwalk. Still, there was no end of opportunity for across-the-board modelling.

Shoe manufacturing and retailing is a very competitive undertaking and my small feet were well suited for fashion shows. These included the BATA Shoe Show held at London's Mayfair Hotel. Having been blessed with small hands too, I was called upon to do much modelling in which my hands were the star of the show.

Never far away were roles as a housewife ironing clothes. Her presence would be off-camera and left in view only her nimble fingers. I hope viewers enjoyed the experience more than I did, as the work was quite arduous. It was often necessary for me to crawl under the ironing board.

My modelling agency was Scotty's, named after its founder, Jean Scott Atkinson, who also mentored her partner, Nigel.

Supposedly a career to die for, modelling work was not particularly well paid. It must be remembered too that modelling is not a regular occupation with a foreseeable salary. For this reason, it was necessary for me to supplement my income by taking a role as a temporary secretary and to be on call for such work. It was in this occupation that I was engaged by Aldwych-based Associated-Rediffusion to carry out work for the business manager, Mr Elms.

As luck would have it, the studio where the famous Sid James TV shows were produced was located downstairs in the basement of the same building. The South-African-born actor was one of Britain's most loved characters. Sid just played himself and he won millions of hearts by doing so. I too was one of his fans. When I heard about the downstairs studio my curiosity and excitement got the better of me and I let my presence be known there. After chatting with the amiable actor, which in itself was an achievement, I was introduced by Sid to the director, who gave me a small part to play.

The fee was a modest £3.15 shillings but the real payoff was that it reignited my burning desire to be an actress. I knew in my heart I could be a winner, although only time and fate can decide this for sure.

Soon afterwards I received a call from my agent. The BBC wanted an unknown actress to work on a twenty-minute project. Whoever was chosen had to accept that the role was unpaid. The feature was an in-house short film for the purpose of helping floor managers to become directors within the BBC. It was directed by a young Indian man called Waris Hussein, who would later direct the first episode of *Doctor Who*.

I jumped at the chance, which was a two-hander with myself and the actor Peter Byrne. My colleague was already engaged as the sidekick to Jack Warner in *Dixon of Dock Green*, which warmed the hearts of Britons throughout the nation. Peter went on to stay in the series as Andy Crawford, moving from a plain old PC to a senior DI, for thirty years.

Then I received another call from my agent. 'Jill, I have good news for you. David Croft, a BBC Director, has seen the part you played in the BBC clip. He wants to interview you about a possible role playing a Cockney girl in the upcoming series *Hugh and I*. If you get the role, you will be in very good company.'

Breathlessly, I asked him who were playing the other roles. My agent told me they were Terry Scott and Hugh Lloyd. Both of these actors were household names and adored by viewers. I was enchanted by the possibility of being included in the cast.

The premise of the show was simple. Terry was a bit of a rogue, basically lazy and always dreaming up get-rich-quick schemes. His character still lived at home with his mother, and invariably dragged their lodger, Hugh, into trying to bring his wild ideas to life with, inevitably, disastrous results. Revolving around all of this were their two sets of neighbours: the elderly Wormolds, and the Crispins, who were out and out snobs. The role I was being considered for was Norma, Mr and Mrs Crispins' young daughter, who always seemed to be being chased by men.

'I would love such a part,' I told my agent. 'Please do what you can to arrange the appointment.'

I sensed his smile as he then told me that it would be necessary for me to adopt a East End accent and demeanour; the series called for a chirpy Cockney sparrow. I was quite good at mimicry, so the interview went well and I secured my dream role. So here I was as a part of the cast of what would become one of Britain's most popular sitcoms, broadcast during prime time at a time when the BBC was attracting its largest audiences ever. The role I played was to last for three series, across four years and some thirty-five shows, and was the ideal showcase for my still budding career as an actress. Due to other commitments, I was unable to return for the third series, but I was welcomed back for the fourth.

David Croft was quietly in charge. He had a gentle and clever way of dealing with people and everyone respected him. He had a terrific vision of how things should go. Towards the end of our weeks' rehearsals of each episode, we would have a run-through, which was always at a church hall, with the flooring marked out with white tape to show where the walls of the sets were. This gave us a rough idea of the space we would be working in and where things were. We would always watch David to see if he approved or not. He never laughed out loud. He would just shake gently and we would know it was OK. He was very talented and went on to create many shows, such as the wonderful *Dad's Army*, still being shown on TV now. The scripts were all by John T Chapman, who'd also had a career as an actor, famously appearing with Brian Rix in a tremendous West End farce called Dry Rot. He played in that for close to 1,500 performances. He certainly got on with Terry, as years later he wrote another hit for him on the BBC called *Happy Ever After*.

After the first series had been completed, we were told a second would be ready to go during the spring of 1963.

However, with only a month or so to go before rehearsals began, the wonderful Cyril Smith, who played Mr Wormold, passed away, and Jack Haig was quickly drafted in, making the part his own very quickly.

Hugh was not really a loner, but he was quite business-like around Terry Scott. Hugh was a quiet soul, who was very gentle and kind, and I liked him very much. Off the set and in the pub, or in the BBC Club, he was good fun. But he also had a kind of shyness which was quite endearing. We had a good rapport and years later, when he had re-married to Shän and was living in Worthing, Leo and I went to visit them and had a wonderful evening. He had just received his MBE from the Queen. Shän, as a journalist, had been helping him with his book *Thank God for a Funny Face*, and he gave me a copy with the inscription: 'Jill, so awful to meet you again, because you haven't changed at all – in other words, you are still smashing and it is lovely to see you and meet lovely Leo, Much Love, Hugh. 7-08-02.'

Terry Scott, conversely, was a good actor but proud. He was a little critical of most of us. He was notorious for handing out notes that specified how he wanted you to change your performance, usually just before you went in front of the cameras! He was dedicated to the job and wanted it all to be perfect. He often bullied actress Patricia Hayes, who had some of the best laughs and was just so nice. But we were all held together by David Croft, who was very diplomatic. Most things were ironed out well. Yes, Terry was analytical, but we worked together well, and I went on to appear with him in *Scott on Birds*. I played the Bride Bird. He, of course, enjoyed a long career and also appeared in a few *Carry On* films.

I was not asked to join the *Carry On* team as I don't think I fitted in. They had already covered all the possible angles for comedy for the ladies. And who could top Barbara Windsor, whom I met at a very funny promotion of the British Safety Council's National Condom Week in Soho at the pub in Old Compton Street.

Television shows were mostly in black-and-white. This was the genesis of an era of iconic television dramas and sitcoms produced by British producers in British studios. There was strong competition from the United States and there must have been some rivalry in the winning of viewers' attentions.

Today, it is about sixty years since the likes of *Dixon of Dock Green*, *The Avengers*, *Dad's Army*, *Steptoe and Son*, and *Thunderbirds*. Fondly recalled are shows such as *Till Death Us Do Part*, *The Saint*, *Z-Cars*, *Armchair Theatre*, *Blue Peter* – oh, so many dramas, sitcoms and television quiz shows. They have not only endured in the nation's memory but their quality and the size of television audiences has never since been bettered.

Competition from across the pond included *I Love Lucy*, *The Twilight Zone*, *Gunsmoke*, *Hawaii Five-O*, *The Flintstones* – again so many. I am surprised that people left their home at night at all!

In the 1970s *Coronation Street*, *Royal Variety Performance* and *To the Manor Born* attracted audiences numbering well over twenty million viewers. To give you an example as to these shows' popularity, the number of people who watched any one of them was more than double today's daily output by Channel 4 and ITV and matched only by the total viewers of all BBC programmes on any given day.

The prospects for aspiring British actors were incredible. There was insatiable demand for there were too few actors and actresses sufficiently well-trained and appropriate for the many roles in programmes being produced.

There was now much for me to learn. Television films and commercials are not so demanding of actors as repertory theatre, where you rehearse a play during the day and perform a different one in the evening, but there is much more to acting than memorising and repeating dialogue. One has to act in accordance with the mores of the period, the mannerisms and the body language, delivery and one's attitude to one's peers. In filming it is essential to be familiar with the camera techniques, the studio equipment and their purpose. One will simply not be a professional actor unless one is familiar with the big studio picture and able to work as a team member with the entire crew.

Hugh and I was part of the continuing evolution of marvellous sitcoms. As time progressed, I was to be cast in several roles produced by the BBC's Light Entertainment Department. I played parts with Peter Cook and Dudley Moore in *Not Only... But Also*, which had become something of a sensation across the country, with the beloved Pete and Dud characters quickly becoming national treasures. I was in the seventh episode of the very first series, appearing alongside the marvellous Eric Sykes as a guest star.

I also appeared in *Hudd*, which was Roy Hudd's sketch show and which was also a ratings success, although it only lasted for one series. I was in the Christmas episode in 1965, alongside the wonderful Dandy Nichols, who was so popular in *Till Death Us Do Part* at the time.

Another comedy legend was Dick Emery, who was an extraordinarily charming man with a perpetual twinkle in his eye, but completely focused and professional to work with. *The Dick Emery Show* ran for years, and I was asked to and agreed to appear with him in late 1967, at the start of his seventh BBC series.

Just as I was making headway in the *Hugh and I* television series my agent pulled me to one side. 'Jill, Walt Disney Studios have been in touch. They will be casting a role in the Disney movie, *Dr. Syn, The Scarecrow of Romney Marsh.*'

This was a 1963 production inspired by a series of novels penned by a Richard Thorndike and first published in 1915. I was, of course, delighted, but also I was aware that there would be much rivalry for the part. I was later to learn that about five hundred actresses had put their name forward for the principal female acting role and about fifty of these aspirants were invited to a screen test.

Being one of those fifty, I suffered a period of anxiety during which time I had to learn to be patient and philosophical. Finally, my agent called to say I had landed the role of Katharine Banks, the squire's daughter. This was incredible news. I was walking on air, pinching myself and wondering if I was dreaming. The news seemed to be unreal, almost surreal. The strange thing is that, after the closing of the screen test, and knowing I had done well, I did have a premonition that I might be favourably considered. David Buck, the actor chosen to play the part of my brother, Harry, had also performed well with me during the female role screen tests. During our ride back to London in the studio's limousine, he had told me that he thought I would be picked to play the part.

Life changed dramatically. First, I had to learn to play the piano-like spinet. This preparation went on for six weeks, during which time I was whisked from dress-fittings, photography sessions and a wide range of other preparations for the making of the actual film. Bear in mind that, during this maelstrom of activity, I was still attending rehearsals and committed to the production of *Hugh and I* weekly. This would have been demanding enough if the show had been pre-recorded, but *Hugh and I* was a live show. Everything was done at the Television Centre at Shepherd's Bush in London. It was effectively like doing live theatre. The shows were recorded in sequence, with an audience sitting on raked seating, watching monitor screens that hung from overhead. The cameras invariably blocked their view of the stage itself as they moved around to get the right shots. Terry was a legendary pantomime dame throughout his career, and knew how to time gags and milk the laughter for all it was worth. In one episode, in particular, there was a car on set. It was an old-fashioned one from the 1920s. We all had to pile in the back, and Terry's reactions as he looked over his shoulder corpsed nearly everyone.

Fortunately, I was chauffeured to and from all the Disney appointments. With great timing, the latest series of *Hugh and I* concluded just as shooting in the Disney Studios commenced. On each shoot, I was tightly laced up in six specially made period dresses. The outfits were made of satin, silk and taffeta and were very beautiful. I believe that still today they are held at Berman's costumiers in London.

I had a 22" waist but, squeezed into a corset or bodice, an hourglass figure was enhanced, giving the impression of a 19" waistline. So attired, it was well-nigh impossible for me to take a seat, and I was provided with a lean-to. This is a wooden structure that you can lean on and rest against between takes. It was also necessary for me to have the lean-to with me in the restaurant where I went with the boys at lunchtime. At times I was propped up against the bar and this I didn't at all mind. The only thing I could manage to eat was a small helping of port-soaked Stilton cheese.

During shooting, we went on location in Rye and we stayed at The Mermaid Inn. The film's story is based on the history of liquor, mainly wine, being smuggled from France into England to avoid ruinous import taxes. The period was that of George III (1760-1801). At night, the boats involved in the smuggling would arrive at the beaches of the Cinque Ports situated along the Kent coastlines. Once beached, the boats would land their illicit cargoes, which were transported in small kegs. The kegs were wheeled along secret tunnels that took them to The Mermaid Inn. The story was based on real-life drama and the hidden staircase leading from the tunnel is still in situ.

The movie starred Patrick McGoohan. He had become incredibly famous thanks to his work on the West End stage, in productions such as *Brand*, and was then riding high on the success of his series *Danger Man*.

There was a romantic side to it, between me as Kate and

Eric Flynn, who was playing the part of a young trooper serving in the King's army. As one might expect, it was all very prim and proper and Father had to approve of the match. There were problems along the way but all turned out right at the end. Indeed, as with most Disney movies, the happy ending saw us married. The whole thing was an incredibly long shoot, as it was being made for Disney's *Walt Disney's Wonderful World of Color* as a three-part series. The idea was to cut its running time down and edit the whole thing together as a film for overseas release, hence it being known as *Dr. Syn, Alias the Scarecrow* outside America.

Patrick played the part of the vicar of Dymchurch but his alternate persona was that of Doctor Syn (alias the Scarecrow). He was the leader of the smugglers but his real identity was unknown. I only knew him as Doctor Syn. He was a very private person and a very good actor. Patrick was an intense and very private person, frighteningly intelligent and he seemed to be acutely aware of every aspect of the filmmaking process. I believe he directed episodes of *Danger Man* and subsequently *The Prisoner*, so his energies were focused on getting an exacting performance on screen. He was never what you'd call sociable, but fine to work with in every regard.

The squire, who was my screen father, was played by Michael Hordern, a very good actor and a genuinely lovely character. In between filming, I would join him and the actor Geoffrey Keen and together we would do the *Sunday Times* crossword. I learned much from these two actors. However, I was not any good at crosswords, so I don't know how much I contributed!

Rye is a very pretty village with much history to rest its case on. Typically English, the location was the perfect setting for the movie. Disney paid for the rebuild and restoration of the parish church that features in the film, as part of the agreement for them to get permission to film there.

A beautiful estate was turned into a movie set and studio. Many of the film stills were taken in the gardens of the Pinewood Estate. I was able to play croquet on the estate's lawns while wearing my period costumes. The crowning glory of this experience occurred one day well into a shooting schedule. Having just completed my take I was leaving the set, and as I did so I met Walt Disney at the door.

'Hello, Jill, how are you? I must say, you are doing a very good job of the part.'

Our encounter was over so quickly, except in my delighted recall. The chance meeting had been so unexpected and brief I was left breathless and wondering whether I had dreamed it. Much later in my life, when I was reading his memoirs, it was mentioned that Walt Disney rarely said a word of praise to any of his actors or other workers in his business. I felt tremendously honoured. Inevitably, one thinks back on the brief encounter and what one would have liked to say goes over and over again in one's mind. But sadly, this was the only occasion I was to meet him.

Some years later, my husband Leo and I visited Rye accompanied by friends. It was especially nice for me to see once again places with which I had once had such great familiarity. We stayed at The Mermaid Inn and after settling into our respective rooms we repaired to the bar. After taking our seats at the inn's enchanting inglenook fireplace, I excused myself and attempted to chat to the then owner-manager.

Lamentably, he was not very receptive. Muttering that it was before his time he displayed not the slightest bit of interest in my movie experiences. In fact, his attitude was so dismissive that his manner verged on the rude. Taken aback, I must admit to being a little shocked and couldn't help wondering what on earth such a man could be doing working in such a historic and divine setting, all of which appeared to be beyond his comprehension.

He had no idea about the secret ladder and subterranean passageways. In fact, he was quite bored with my telling him about these very special features relating to his otherwise charming inn. Oh well, such is life – and lack of life.

I suppose one could say in diary terms that 1963 was the year of *Dr. Syn*. By this time Derek had purchased a semi-detached house in London's Little Venice and had moved from our shared home in Mayfair. From then on we slept separately. The kitchen and the living room were situated on the middle floor and our respective bedrooms were on the top and bottom floors.

CHAPTER TEN
HAMPSTEAD AND MAIDA VALE

NOW, WITH one car and two homes, I had a little more independence. The theory was fine, but the practice was arduous, to say the least. Keeping two places going at the same time was like chasing fool's gold, and a useless demand on time and cost. My weeks of supposed relaxation in the rustic idyll were spent cleaning and tidying up the gardens as the cost of servants were beyond our means. Our cottage in Penshurst had already proven a luxury too far and the money from its sale had gone into the new apartment in Little Venice.

But life goes on and my career was keeping me much occupied. Derek and I became ships that occasionally passed in the night. However, I was still keen on shooting and still attended events in various parts of Britain and France during special weekends.

After the Disney movie premiered in London, with all the razzmatazz that accompanies such events, the movie was put on general release. It was then that I was called upon to help promote the movie in different parts of England. Admittedly, it was rather splendid to be chauffeur driven and riding high, either in an Austin Princess or a Rolls Royce saloon. Dressed in my period costume, I was accompanied by the studio's public relations manager, John Foster. During these excursions, we two became firm friends.

I recall coming out of Claridge's Hotel in London. Ahead of me was the lengthy red carpet stretching to the movie company's waiting limousine. As I flounced down the aisle, I was approached by a youngster who enquired if he might have my autograph. Chatting briefly, he told me his name was David Hemmings. Yes, he was the very same who later became a film producer, but at the time he was simply a very young film fan. His sensational performance in *Blow Up*, for director Michelangelo Antonioni, was only a couple of years away.

On reaching the car and stepping inside the saloon, I realised the unusual lack of light was due to the number of people peering through the limo's windows. Some fans were clambering over the car's bonnet, roof and boot to get a better view of me. I recall, in particular, the squeaking sound of fingers running down the limousine's bodywork. I found it quite intimidating, but keeping his cool the chauffeur eased out into the traffic and sped off without anyone being hurt.

This was my first taste of fame and my first experience of being hemmed in by a crowd of excited strangers. I was frightened by the experience and determined to avoid such incidents in the future wherever possible.

Our stay in our new home in Little Venice was short-lived as it didn't suit either of us very well. Derek bought a new apartment in Hampstead. Our neighbours there included Peter Sellers, who was living with Britt Ekland. He was easy to spot when he zoomed off in his gold-plated Mini, which for such a small car had an astronomical price tag! Jackie Collins had an apartment there too.

These were attractive and very spacious apartments set in a park. Each had very large picture windows and lovely fittings. Derek and I lived on the one level, and again we had our separate bedrooms and bathrooms.

At the time of our moving from Riverside, I had the presence of mind to bring with me some weeping willow saplings. Having brought them to London I bedded them into their new home at Martlet Lodge. Sadly, two saplings didn't survive but one did. When I re-visited our old home many years later it brought me great joy to see the weeping willow had matured into a truly beautiful tree.

I loved Hampstead. I had been born there and now it was the perfect place for an upwardly mobile actress to be in situ. I was surrounded by so many interesting people. I recall with great fondness Peter Cook, Dudley Moore, Norman Rossington, and Ronnie Fraser, affectionately called Moonface.

Close by there were the many iconic pubs and restaurants, the watering holes of the avant-garde like the Le Cellier du Midi. There were also small arty theatres where new writers and directors would try out their new plays. I suppose all aspired to have their names in lights across London's West End.

Ours was a very comforting and I suppose village-like atmosphere and yet bustling London was but such a short distance away. The village atmosphere was a little too quiet for me. I preferred the more vibrant hang-on-to-my-coat-tails London city centre. It was important for me to be as close to the action as possible. I needed to be close to the centre to attend interviews and photo shoots; here too, in the centre of the metropolis, were situated the television world's studios. The 'village' was better suited for writers like Jackie Collins or established stars like Peter Sellers, as their being creative individuals they needed space and quiet.

The ever-creative Derek liked Martlet Lodge. Inclined to be reclusive, he was in harmony with his surroundings. Derek never touched alcohol, chit-chat bored him and he far preferred the solitude of the office, where, free of distractions, he could seek to advance his career. In many ways, my husband wasn't so much a misfit as perhaps unfitted for the social environment. Certainly he was gregarious in unavoidable situations, but friends and acquaintances, situations and opportunities tended to be screened in or out as he wished them to be. Otherwise, like his American mother, his personal charm only shone brightly when the social occasion called for it, and his conviviality dimmed soon afterwards. This in itself is not a bad thing of course.

Eventually, he sold Martlet Lodge and we opted for renting two flats in Stuart Tower in Maida Vale. That was fine by me: this location was much closer to the West End. My apartment was on the fourth floor while Derek's was situated higher on the eleventh floor. At his suggestion, we were connected by a walkie-talkie arrangement so we could chat without interrupting our telephone connections, which were constant and important. It was still vital that we share much of our lives. Whatever our differences we were still a couple who relied upon each other in many ways, not all of which were career-fixated.

I suppose we were what the Victorians called romantic friends. We were confidants who trusted each other and knew that we could confide in each other our innermost feelings without fear of compromise. Derek was always taken up discussing issues of importance to him. I found my time was fast changing into his time and I was playing second fiddle to my husband's needs. It was time for me to self-focus.

CHAPTER ELEVEN
DIVORCE AND NICKY HENSON

OUR MARRIAGE was now one of some convenience, but whose convenience? Surely not mine. Being better able to see our situation from a distance, and fuelled by my need for self-preservation, I felt that I really wanted to get on. I finally realised that divorce was the only answer. Filing my request for divorce, I did so under the adultery clause. The evidence of the sin was self-evident and freely offered and all was finalised in the London court. This occurred in 1966 while I was very much involved in rehearsing and filming a hit television series, *Quick Before They Catch Us*.

The premise was so simple; a gang of three teenagers race around London in the swinging '60s, solving crimes and having adventures. It was an instant hit with viewers when it was broadcast, but for reasons that are long lost in time, the BBC decided to stop making it after just one series.

On the day of my divorce, they stopped filming my scene, I took a taxi to appear in the London court, and an hour later took a taxi back to Notting Hill market to finish filming!

Regrets about our marriage and divorce were few, if any. Ours had never been a marriage in the conventional sense.

Nevertheless, it was a sad ending as Derek had brought much of my life to me. It was to this backdrop that, when the papers arrived to inform me of my new and independent status, I felt as though I was in some kind of vacuum. The sense of loss was carried over to the scene in which I played that day. This filmed drama had by chance a similarly sad storyline. I am sure I carried the scene through with greater empathy as a consequence of my sense of personal loss.

I otherwise felt liberated, which ironically is a condition that frees one up to lose one's freedom to another party. I had now a deep-seated yearning for a more meaningful relationship.

About two years earlier, I had become acquainted and then friendly with a budding actor. Nicky Henson was a natural thespian. I was captivated by Nicky and I knew also of his father, who was none other than the great vaudeville artiste Leslie Henson. Nicky and I eventually became lovers and we two were inseparable. The problem was the fact that I still had my home in Stuart Tower while Nicky's home was in Kings Road, and we had to alternate between the two domiciles.

A girl head over heels in love and with London at my feet! My evenings were spent at the Phoenix Theatre in the West End, where I was performing in *Monsieur Blaise*, a French farce. I played a Spanish girl called Pepita and spoke entirely in Spanish. It was quite a challenge but it was a good part in a strong piece of work and the play ran for six months. It had toured around England, from Bristol to Brighton and then Blackpool, before settling for an initial month-long stay at the Royal Court Theatre. We then moved to the Phoenix Theatre down Charing Cross Road. It had been directed by its lead, Jimmy Thompson, who had become a star in farces since the early '50s. He formed a tight knit team with his wife, who had adapted *Monsieur Blaise*, and the whole thing went at a frantic pace.

We dined at Gerry's during the evenings or at The

Buckstone. We danced the night away at whichever of the nightspots suited our mood. Occasionally we would be found at The Pickwick, where we met the Beatles, or at the Ad-Lib, Brads or a few others of preference.

Nicky too was working hard and there was much for him to be involved in. He was with Lawrence Harvey in *Camelot* playing Mordred and later in several other musicals. As if that wasn't enough, Nicky, being a good vocalist and excellent guitarist, was often called upon as a key part of the group, which also starred Ian Ogilvy and Paul Ferris.

Grass was never left to grow under Nicky's feet. He was also a motorcycling enthusiast. He owned a Norton motorcycle, which like Triumph Motorcycles was a bike that had quite a following. For aficionados, these two British bikes almost outclassed America's Harley-Davidsons. I often rode a pillion but being of a rather cautious nature I much preferred my safer Austin Healey Sprite. One could still enjoy the breeze combing one's hair as one pelted through England's country lanes without the risks of a motorbike.

I recall in particular a delightful solo drive that took me up the new M1 motorway to Birmingham, where Nicky was appearing in *Entertaining Mr Sloane*. My boyfriend was also a regular on the very popular television production *That Was the Week That Was*, in which he starred with David Frost and John Cleese.

Another of our favourite watering holes was the Trattoria Terraza, situated on Romilly Street in Soho. I recall arriving there with Nicky one night. After parking my Sprite, I was unprepared for a pleasing surprise when Larry Harvey clambered out of my car's boot. Nicky had offered him a lift after the performance in *Camelot*. Larry had very sportingly squeezed into the back of my car.

It was such great fun and we giggled as we made our way to the table where David Frost, John Cleese, Roy Kinnear, and their girlfriends were sitting. Being regulars at

Trattoria Terraza in Soho, we were close friends with the upmarket restaurant's owners, the Mario and Franco brothers. We were dubbed the 'crazy show business bunch'. El Tiberio, the couple's other restaurant, was to be discovered in Mayfair's Chesterfield Street. This eatery was a favourite of Judy Garland and a favourite of ours too.

One can be excused for thinking of how ostentatious and expensive such restaurants must have been. But looking back it is amazing how reasonably priced and indeed affordable they were. It has to be remembered that, back in the 1960s, actors were not well paid. Sure, stars were surrounded by glamour; they were photographed in the most splendid hotels and resorts while wearing expensive clothes and jewels. Stars were seen coming and going in limousines, but the cost was borne by their agencies or studios and was never out of their own modest incomes. Of course, it was different in America, where they were paid much more.

The same could be said of sports stars and football managers, who lived in ordinary houses. It was a good thing really as it helped to keep our feet on the ground, rather than floating over the heads of our equally hard-working fans and viewers. Interestingly, whomsoever I chat with from that era now, regardless of their career or social background, we always have two things in common: we were quite low paid yet they were the best days of our lives.

Ours was a vibrant way of life that provided plenty of openings for entrepreneurs to provide for followers of the 'good life'. New membership clubs were opening and fees were affordable and offered very good value for money. We received free or low fee memberships as our presence reflected well on their business.

Their popularity was due to the fact that, if you were a licensee of a privately owned club, you could get around the prohibitive alcohol-related laws and obtain the necessary license for the purchase of all legal alcohol drinks. Both the

British movie and television industries were firing on all cylinders and there was a constant demand for new actors and established household thespians to sign up as members.

This theatrical village, if I can describe it like that, was a very small and friendly community. We all either knew or were aware of each other, and the bonhomie among us was empowering. London back then was quite different from what it has since become, and so a tale of two cities indeed. Yes, there was serious crime, but very much in a different world than what we see today. Apart from having to read about it in the newspapers, crime simply wasn't an issue for most people.

Those who in a manner of speaking had achieved what is now regarded as celebrity status were familiar faces in the restaurants, pubs and clubs.

The Village (Club) on Lower Sloane Street was a favourite haunt with the models, agents and photographers. But actor and actress members were thin on the ground. Alex Stirling ran the latter very well. His club was chic, friendly, and as one might expect, the club's members, while being something of a clique, were otherwise outgoing and friendly.

Alex had another club situated in Kings Road. This venue was named The Pheasantry. It was situated in a lovely old house with its front gardens and steps leading up to the front door. Regency period columns graced its entrance. In truth, the club looked a little out of place as it was set in a street that was otherwise quite ordinary and few had ornate entrances. The club seemed to resist change as other shops were at this time hastily modernising their facades.

The club itself was austere and upmarket and many thought it lacked atmosphere. It was a tad different in that most clubs not requiring a high-profile frontage were situated in basements. The basement offered a unique sense of smoky intimacy. Those who patronised basement clubs could feel as though they had stepped off the hamster wheel of life. There was a liveliness to be enjoyed and somehow it felt as if clocks were a thing of the past. Of course, such basement clubs were artificially lit as there were no windows, but this added to the timelessness of evenings spent there.

One very upmarket club was The Saddle Room, situated just down from the Hilton Hotel in Park Lane. This was glitzy yet intimate, with small and square black leather upholstered stools and leather banquettes. I recall one night in particular when Richard Harris and his wife arrived in the company of some friends. Quite early on in the evening, Richard declared that he was bored. 'Let's go somewhere else,' he suggested. 'My car's outside.'

About eight of us headed for the club's door and outside was his Rolls Royce with its chauffeur. After we had all tumbled inside the saloon, the car took off to Brads in Jermyn Street. I must say, it wasn't the most comfortable of rides. Despite it being a big car, there were eight of us, and all were in high spirits.

Richard was in great form and thankfully had enough of his wits about him not to drive himself. To be honest, I have no idea where we all ended up that night. I recall hazily that we were dancing until the wee small hours. After the party was over, I took a taxi and arrived home either very late at night or very early in the morning; it hardly seemed to matter which as I tumbled into bed. This was 1961, the time we were renting our apartment at the bottom of Curzon Street, where my stage name found its inspiration.

I often strolled up Curzon Street towards Park Lane until I came to number twenty-eight, located on the left-hand side of the street. Here was to be found The White Elephant Club, which at that time was owned by Victor Brusa and his wife Stella Richman, a television producer.

After I had become one of the club's founder members, most days would find me sipping a pre-lunch drink after others had retired to the restaurant for lunch. Nino, the barman, would seduce me with a plate of smoked salmon, lemon and chopped onion. Thereupon, I would place myself comfortably in a corner of the bar with a glass of white wine; I was never charged for the salmon.

The White Elephant Club became my local. I got on well with the club's Italian waiters, Ronaldo, Orlando and others I remember with great affection. True professionals, the staff waiting on us invariably made me feel as if I were a royal patron.

As Derek never took me out, I was flying solo. For this reason, I was often to be found eating on my own at The White Elephant, but surrounded with such friendliness and familiarity, I never felt as if I was on my own. Naturally I did make many friends. The club was a favourite of John Kennedy, who was our landlord too. He liked meeting his clients at The White Elephant and I got to know them all, television and theatre producers and directors. Often to be seen was Vidal Sassoon, Tommy Yeardye, and Eric Steiner accompanied by his wife Lynn Peters, who eventually became the owner of The Pair of Shoes Gambling Club upstairs.

I didn't have what might be called a close friendship with anyone and in a way I was something of a loner. Comfortable in my own skin, I didn't feel the need to share my life with anyone else, even a girlfriend. Well used to the social scene, I visited clubs, pubs or anywhere that took my fancy. It was I supposed the ultimate freedom, being answerable to no one but myself.

I lived the best of both worlds, as when and where circumstances allowed there were plenty of opportunities for me to socialise and, if not make friends, then to make acquaintances. I had several women associates loosely termed friends but they were strong and independent, self-sufficient ambitious females like Diana Dors.

My friends included a wonderful Eurasian lady named Eileen Allison. Eileen ran the Stockport Restaurant opposite the Comedy Theatre off Leicester Square. She was a marvellous cook with a vivacity that was compelling. My friend eventually sold up and placed London in her rear-view mirror. Her preferred self-exile was Ibiza in the company of Carlos Vico, a classical guitarist who was a Spaniard. The couple were to have a beautiful daughter, Lara.

Their restaurant was called La Villa and waiting to be discovered in Santa Eulalia. Nearby was the couple's farm with the ever-present family horse, whose name was Confiado. Far better than the television horse Mister Ed, Confiado achieved some kind of fame in his own right. Confiado featured in a book penned by Carlos, *The Unknown Ibiza*. We have stayed in touch and I visited Eileen years later with Michelle, who was the same age as my friend's daughter, Lara.

Another who remained a good friend was my college pal Anne Houlbrooke-Bowers. Anne had stayed with Elizabeth Arden for some years during which time she had met and married her long-time friend Mike Houlbrooke. We lost touch when Anne went to the United States for some years.

Meanwhile, life on the boards was going very much the way I had hoped it would. There were many calls on my time, and some really pleasing roles in television drama were now coming my way. It is such a pleasure to be so enthusiastic about one's work that one never looks forward to going home. I was cast for a main part in *Mrs Quilley's Murder Shoes*, and I was working with the wonderful Irish actor Milo O'Shea and director Peter Collinson. I cannot forget working with the outrageous Fenella Fielding on this, who adored her lush marine-blue velvet dress and hat, and swanned around with her feather boa as though she'd just walked out of the 1920s. And for reasons that I can't recall, we also had a live cow in the studio. It had scenes with Fenella and frequently tried to upstage her!

Also special to me were the French director Henri

Saffran, and Michael Mills, director of *The World of Wooster* starring Ian Carmichael and Dennis Price, in which I played the part of Gwladys, the mad artist from Chelsea.

The first series had been a tremendous success. This episode was for the second series. It was called *Jeeves and a Spot of Art*. Ian really went for it as an upper class twit, characterising Bertie Wooster with a stammer and sublime stupidity, whereas Dennis played Jeeves with a world weary calmness that was almost droll, yet had an air of mystery about him that was very cleverly done. Poor Dennis got into terrible financial difficulties and ended up moving to Sark, which was a tax haven. He was perfectly charming and witty, but seemed quite a lonely man.

The part entailed my driving around Belgrave Square in a 1920s bright yellow Lagonda open-top saloon, the controls of which I had to learn. It was very nearly final curtains for Ian Carmichael. The renowned actor was much relieved when I pulled to a stop inches from him. It was Ian's lucky day, for his being knocked down was actually in the script. He fell by himself, and it all worked out fine, but he had been incredibly apprehensive beforehand and had to trust my ability!

On the verge of my being overwhelmed by wonderful opportunities, I decided to quit *Hugh and I*. I had been a key member of the cast for four years, and that was something of a marathon. Wendy Richard took over my part and she took the production to the end of the series. Wendy went on to *Are You Being Served* and *Eastenders*. These parts were made for her. Unlike me, the popular actress was born and bred Cockney, and had no need to act the persona as I did.

In spring 1965 I was cast in *The Saint* in a wonderful guest role. Thinking back, you couldn't avoid Simon Templer and his adventures. Leslie Chateris had published so many stories. The story I appeared in came from a volume of short stories called *The Saint on the Spanish Main*. Sadly, I didn't go on an exotic location trip with Roger

Moore. I played a mysterious Spanish lady called Maria Cavallini, and the furthest I got from England was the Elstree Film Studios. Roger had been all over the world on screen, but never actually left the studio back lot.

Did you know that Roger claimed to have invented Wall's Magnum? He would say, 'The person I'd like to meet more than anyone else is Mr Walls, of Wall's Ice Cream, and ask him why he doesn't sell a choc ice on a stick?' This apparently inspired Wall's to do just this. Apparently Roger had always put them on sticks as a child, and thought it would be a wonderful product.

As to whether this is actually true, who knows? He had so many wild stories to tell. And he also liked to draw. One of the walls in the studios at Elstree was like an old school blackboard. Roger would draw cartoons and caricature with chalk there. He was a lovely man, and so much fun to work with. I believe he did close to one hundred and twenty episodes of *The Saint* in the end!

The ITC adventure and thriller shows were part of a production line, a nonstop conveyor belt churning out product. They were also guaranteed to reach an audience in the USA, which was great for potential casting awareness. And as for Roger Moore himself, I hate to shatter any illusions about him being suave and sophisticated, but behind the scenes he was a big kid with a unique sense of humour.

CHAPTER TWELVE
A MOVIE STAR AND MEETING KING HUSSEIN

MY FIRST film wasn't, in fact, the Walt Disney production. Before that memorable role, Val Guest picked me to play Nurse Jill in *80,000 Suspects*. My co-stars were Claire Bloom and Richard Johnson. The story centred on a smallpox infection that plagued Bath in Somerset during which epidemic the entire population of the city was quarantined. This proclamation would stay in place until every man, woman and child had been vaccinated. It was an interesting experience and most of the scenes were night scenes and I recall it being very cold outside.

While on location we stayed at the Lansdown Grove Hotel in the middle of Bath. This gave us ample opportunity to get to know the city, without of course any risk of our catching smallpox. Claire Bloom's husband, Rod Steiger, accompanied her through some of the movie production and he was quite high-spirited in character. Astonishingly, there was one morning when, for no other reason than his being bored, he leapt up and jumped about on the hotel's freshly made-up breakfast tables.

Richard Johnson and I became firm friends. He was a very funny man with an intriguing sense of humour that tended to be unexpected. He was so amiable. We two often dined at the Hole in the Wall restaurant. Clare was not too happy about my dining with Richard, who was her leading man, as it was the unspoken protocol that the leading man at all times dined with the leading lady.

During our chats, I learned that he was a professional classical actor who had parts in Shakespeare productions in Stratford-upon-Avon. At the time, my friend and colleague was also penning an adaptation of *The Devils*. He was very much enamoured of Julie Christie but I am not sure his ardour was returned. I also recall that we filmed in Bath during appalling weather. It was absolutely freezing, and there were so many extras. Giant heaters, braziers I think, were positioned out of shot along the streets to try and keep everyone warm, and there were problems with snow. It just wouldn't thaw, so a decision had to be made to keep going despite the weather.

Then there was another part in a low budget thriller called *Smokescreen* for director Jim O'Connolly, who also came up with the script. The lead actors were Peter Vaughn, who could always play sinister wonderfully but in this film played a comedic part as an insurance investigator, and John Carson, whose rich velvety voice led him to (vocally) being compared to James Mason. My character was called June.

We filmed in Sussex, mainly around Brighton, and in the end, for a B movie, it turned out rather well and got good reviews. I understand that even today it's well regarded by, amongst others, the British Film Institute.

Later that year, I worked with Morecambe and Wise on television in an episode of *Two of a Kind*. There was a palpable change in dynamic when they moved to the BBC, as they had Eddie Braben writing for them, but when I worked with them they had the ever present Sid Green and Dick Hills working on their scripts.

I also worked with Morecambe and Wise on a special variety show called *Piccadilly Palace*. It was their attempt to break into the US market. As a result, a very strange thing happened. A fight broke out between the cameramen. You see, it was being filmed for both the UK and the USA, and there were two separate crews. Because the American team were filming in colour, they got pole position for the angles, and the UK cameras had to literally stand alongside them and record in black-and-white. So truthfully speaking, ATV (the UK broadcaster) were getting short-changed. In that regard, it was all a bit odd!

There was a very funny sketch in which Eric played a French artist busy painting a model, that part being played by me. My charms were covered only by a white sable fur coat, but underneath I was actually wearing a bikini. A security guard had been engaged to keep an eye on the set. He was told he could take his eyes off me but not off the expensive sable fur. The guard followed me everywhere except the ladies' room, where he waited outside!

I also appeared in several Morecambe and Wise feature films, the first being *The Intelligence Men*, a spoof on James Bond. As the opening titles rise to a backdrop of French music, you see me in bed looking like the cat that has just had the cream. Then, as the cameras roll, I turn towards my screen lover, whom the viewers don't see. But, in my horror, I leap from the bed with appropriate sticking plaster over my lady-bits as I grab for my nightgown and the telephone to call the police. It is then that the audience learns that a famous private-eye operative has 'died on active duty to Her Majesty the Queen'.

The Magnificent Two was my second film in which I had the chance to work with Britain's most loved comedians. I played the part of an officer in the Women's Army. Incongruously, our uniform included a woven image of a red lace bikini and we trim ladies carried assault rifles. This movie was an absolute farce and was the greatest of fun to be in.

Morecambe and Wise were super fun all the time. They

never stopped their nonsense together, and it was a bit like no one else was really there at all. They had an incredible bond between them, and they were always busy thinking up the next joke. Working with them you were always the third person, and they often made up their dialogue on the spot, like when I played the 'Artist Model in the Sable Coat'. I didn't particularly socialise with them, except when they came to Spain with their wives and stayed at the Los Monteros Hotel in Marbella. We went to meet them then, and their wives were very nice. They were good friends and both accepted their slightly mad husbands.

This was only the second time in my acting career that I had been one of a group of ladies. On the first occasion, I had been just eight years old, when I performed with similarly aged girls at the World of Health & Beauty Club of Great Britain. This was a memorable occasion since our local group in Surrey was selected to perform at the Albert Hall.

We had performed many exercise routines dressed in white satin blouses and black satin shorts, and our wear on that second occasion included red tap-dancing shoes decorated with little red bows. The tap-dancing routines were very enjoyable and made us all very proud of the roles we had played. Yet, as my stage career progressed, the Morecambe and Wise movie was the only time since that I had performed as part of a female troupe.

Also at The Albert Hall was *Easter Parade*, in which, as a little girl, I had been dressed as a chicken. Imagine! I was covered from head to foot in yellow feathers, wearing also a chicken head mask sporting a very long beak. All us children loved it as did presumably the parents at the shows.

Hugh and I had provided me with great training and experiences which would be to my benefit in roles yet to be played. When working at Television Centre, we used old church halls for our rehearsals. I must say that these buildings were extremely cold during England's long winters. They were impossible to heat by conventional means. In these rehearsal halls, there was just a single urn that provided for the heating of hot water for our tea and coffee. Looking back, one supposes that even the most popular television shows and dramas were produced on a shoestring budget and filmed under the most austere conditions.

That first morning of rehearsal we gathered and got our heads around the new script personally brought by our own writer, John Chapman. Sitting around the trestle table we all familiarised ourselves with it. It was always fun to read through new plots and at such an early stage to imagine actually playing our parts. The rest of the week was spent plotting the layout and marking the floor with tape for our respective positions.

Taking lunch breaks in a nearby pub we were refuelled by sandwiches. There were sausages, scotch eggs and a nice glass of whatever we fancied. Less than an hour was taken because we simply wanted to get on with what we were paid to do.

The technicians from the BBC turned up on a Friday and we went through our paces to assist them in setting up the lighting and camera positions. These lovely guys were enjoying a preview of what the viewers would hopefully soon be relishing. They were a great barometer. They joined in the spirit of the show and they gave us inspiration, especially when what we thought amusing also tickled them. This was especially important as the show was to be filmed the next day and with a live audience in Television Centre. Our director, David Croft used to say, 'If the technicians laugh then we have a show.'

During BBC shows we always had a 'warm-up' comedian who came on stage before us. His job was to get the audience relaxed and in the mood to laugh whatever was to come. The show was then recorded for its BBC television screening. This would usually take place about two weeks after the live show.

After the show, the usual practice was to retire to the BBC club before going home. In the bar and restaurant, we would meet family or friends who we had invited to the club. After which, on occasion, we decided to go on to the Angus Steak House. This was underneath Stuart Tower in Maida Vale and was convenient for me as this was my home too.

I was a member of the BBC Television Centre club for several years. After my contract for *Hugh and I* ended I could not renew my membership and I felt something of a loss. The club itself was mainly a watering hole for those working in the administration department and we thespians were tolerated. The understanding was that we recognised their pre-eminence and accepted that we were less equal than the others. My next visit to the BBC club wouldn't happen until I landed my next job with the corporation.

One Saturday I remember with mixed feelings. I was preparing for a final run-through on *Hugh and I* and the show was to be screened that very night. During the frenzied activity, I was provided with a shotgun and perched in appropriate settings for publicity shots. These were destined for the news media, and prominent in the photos were Hugh Lloyd and Terry Scott.

You can imagine my expression when the session was interrupted by the entrance of none other than King Hussein of Jordan. His visit was so unexpected that I was momentarily taken aback. There had been no warning at all. The king was brought to me in a beeline. As introductions and pleasantries were exchanged I was told that he had watched and liked the shows and had made a point of asking to be introduced to me. To say that I was astounded is an understatement!

While trying to keep my composure I made an attempt at a curtsy, which turned out to be more of a cutesy! As he took my hand, he chatted in perfect English and complimented me on my role in the show. Something of a shotgun enthusiast, he had heard that I was a bit of an Annie Oakley, and we chatted amiably about our shared interest. After a few further pleasantries and the king's departure, I was pinching myself. After that performance, changing tack and returning to my role was even more of a challenge. My father later told me the king was an ex-Sandhurst man.

I later learned that at this time he was looking for a wife. In the end, he was to find her and subsequently married his Queen Noor, the daughter of an American journalist who was a friend of King Hussein. I have always treasured that gem of a moment in my life and career. It was a terrific boost to my ego to realise that I was one he had considered in his quest for matrimonial bliss.

Another charming memory from *Hugh and I* stems from one of our Christmas shows, when I was about to sing a song especially written for me.

The ballad was called 'Sooty Santa'. It was a light-hearted story about Santa coming down the chimney. The sketch's songwriter was the incredibly talented John Barry. Many will remember John as being one of the John Barry Seven, and he also went on to compose the James Bond theme. I hope my voice did his composition justice. I do so wish I had a copy or a recording as it was a treasured moment for me.

The Riviera Police, filmed in France, saw John Meillon as a racing driver and me as his wife called Jenny, keeping account of his lap times on my stopwatch. The whole thing was set against the backdrop of the Monaco Grand-Prix. He was great to work with and became a good friend. He later returned to his native Australia where he mostly played in theatre, but he had one very famous part of the Adjutant in *Crocodile Dundee*, which was really his swansong. He was a lovely, funny character. Sadly, the show only lasted one series, but something for *Doctor Who* fans to note was that I appeared alongside Nicholas Courtney, who was later to become so well-known as the beloved Brigadier Lethbridge-Stewart.

I heard that the ratings for the first episode were huge but then plummeted, and even though it followed the cultural icon that is *Coronation Street* each week, the viewers didn't continue to tune in.

I was a guest on *The Roy Hudd Show* but made no appearance in *On the Braden Beat* despite being paid for it. Then there was *Dee Time*. Simon Dee was a cultural phenomenon, who shone so brightly and then seemed to just vanish from the scene. He had the most extraordinary real name, Cyril Nicholas Henty-Dodd, and was one of the original DJs with Radio Caroline. The BBC soon grabbed him and put him on air, and by 1967 he had *Dee Time*, his own TV chat show.

I flew to Manchester to be interviewed on air by him. He co-incidentally had a flat in Stuart Tower, but we didn't socialise. I was too busy with Nicky Henson.

Simon's extravagant lifestyle was all over the headlines, and he could regularly be seen being driving around Kings Road in a silver Aston Martin. After about three years, his bubble burst allegedly due to him asking for more money from the BBC, and he was rarely seen again.

Nicky and I were really good dancing partners, and we would always get up on the stage and do our thing for hours on end. Where did we get all that energy? One of our favourite places was the Pickwick Club, made famous by Harry Secombe, who played Mr Pickwick. The Beatles also liked to go there for dinner with their spouses.

Nicky appeared at the London Palladium, with Harry Secombe topping the bill, at the end of their season in November 1967. Nicky and I were invited to join Harry and his family on a trip to the newly independent country of Barbados, where we spent Christmas together. Harry had just made the recording of his song 'If I Ruled the World', which was an amazing, lovely hit. He was a marvellous man and had a great family. We loved him and had a simply wonderful holiday. Barbados had a Nelson's Column in the centre of Bridgetown which was older than ours in Trafalgar Square! We whizzed around the island and its sugar plantations on Nicky's hired moped. The weather and food were divine and so was the Mountgay Rum! Great memories.

I had many odd jobs, like a YEB (Yorkshire Electric Board) commercial for TV and cinema, followed by voice looping and hand modelling. I also did *The Terry Scott Show*. My episode was 'Scott on Birds', in which I played the bride bird getting undressed for bed while the husband remained disinterested. They had to cut before I took too many clothes off. It was very funny but puritanical, although daring for those days. Then there was *The Dave Allen Show*, for which I was paid but ended up not being used!

I also did a lot of voiceovers, which were amazingly paid at the time.

In late 1967, Don Sharp, who had directed Hammer Films, and worked a lot with Christopher Lee, hired me to play an air stewardess in *The Champions*. This was another ITC series. Directors like Don would do these jobs between movies. It was a frantic schedule. They would shoot quick set ups and rattle through scripts in a matter of days. The finished results usually looked ten times better than the budget suggested they would.

This series starred the wonderful William Gaunt, Stuart Damon and Alexandra Bastedo, who I believe was dating Omar Sharif at the time. This was her big break, and although she went on to play leads in films and other series, she eventually focused her time on saving stray animals, and wound up running a sanctuary with her eventual husband, the theatre director Patrick Garland.

Also there was *Carnival Time* for Anglia TV. This was a very strange gameshow, shot by one of the regional TV stations, Anglia. Bob Monkhouse hosted the studio recording with a guest panel of judges, while the DJ Pete Murray was out with an outside broadcast unit. I think the rules eluded us, the viewers and everyone else, because nobody watched it, and nobody remembers it, including me, and I was there!

The director John Paddy Carstairs asked for me as I had worked with him before. He also wrote two books which he signed for me. He was a funny little livewire of a man and very talented in directing in his own style.

Another photographer and writer was Philip Gotlop, who chose me to go on the cover of his photography book, which taught how to light in different climates and conditions. He was of international repute, having photographed Marilyn Monroe and The Beatles, so I was very proud he chose me to pose for one of his covers. It was a PAN book, and they seemed to like me after all the covers I had posed for them in the past.

Another fun show I worked on in 1967 was *The Des O'Connor Show,* produced again by John Paddy Carstairs, which we did in Bournemouth, plus some film sequences in Elstree with Frankie Vaughan, Malcolm Roberts, Jack Parnell and his Orchestra and the Mike Sammes Singers.

In October I was asked to be at the opening of a boutique in Belfast called Vivienne McMaster. I was flown there with Bob Monkhouse and a model friend of mine, Ivi King, there and back in one day. I remember quite a lot of wine was drunk by all, but it was fun and we were paid for it.

In January 1967, I was cast in *Adam Adamant Lives!* starring the wonderful Gerald Harper in the title role. It was very much like the BBC's version of *The Avengers*, so it was back to TV Centre for a day of studio rehearsal, and then recording the following day just before Valentine's Day! I played an exotic temptress called Juanita. I love the fact that Gerald wore false eyebrows as Adam, and that when the series finished he was presented with them framed with an inscription underneath, which read, 'Here Lies the Eyebrows of Adam Adamant'.

I seem to recall the stunt men being very brave with the

sword fighting as well, as Gerald was rather short-sighted, and took his glasses off just before each take. I can only think there was an awful lot of rehearsing beforehand!

Later that month, I was on *The Dick Emery Show* for the BBC, which was really funny. Dick was certainly a man with an eye for the ladies, a rogue with a twinkle in his eye. You'd see him arrive at rehearsals and the studios on a gigantic motor bike that looked far too big for him. Next to the ladies, racing bikes was Dick's main passion. The great actor Sir Ralph Richardson was the same about motor bikes, and you'd see him around theatre land in London waving cheerily, but unlike Dick, Ralph liked to drive with his pet parrot on his shoulders.

Also on *The Dick Emery Show* were Patsy Rowlands and singer Anita Harris, who was a good friend, and Stratford Johns. This was in colour – one of the first – and so good for export to the States. Then Royant cast me in a clay pigeon film, and I was paid with 1,000 cartridges – very useful!

By now I had enough performances behind me that I was getting repeat fees. My last job was on January 5th 1968, and partly shot in Notting Hill Market; it was an episode of *Market in Honey Lane*, which was a very successful series starring John Bennett, Peter Birral, Ray Lonnen, Ivor Salter, Vicki Woolf and Pat Nye. It was an atmospheric soap opera that strove to be kitchen sink drama. And I had a lovely part in it.

A young Jill Curzon, 1939.

Toddler Jill on the steps, 1940.

Jill, Mum and Dad, 1941.

Jill and Mum, 1942.

Four-year-old Jill with doll, 1943.

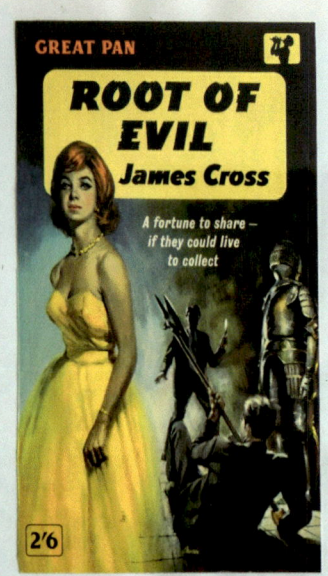
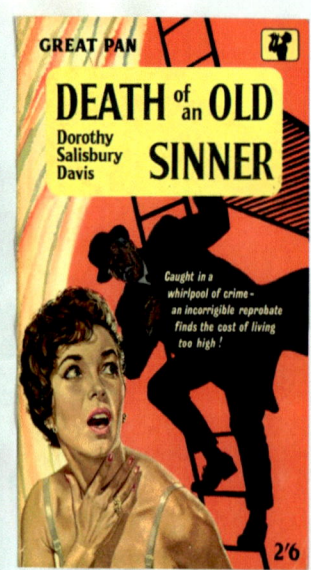

Four Pan book covers.

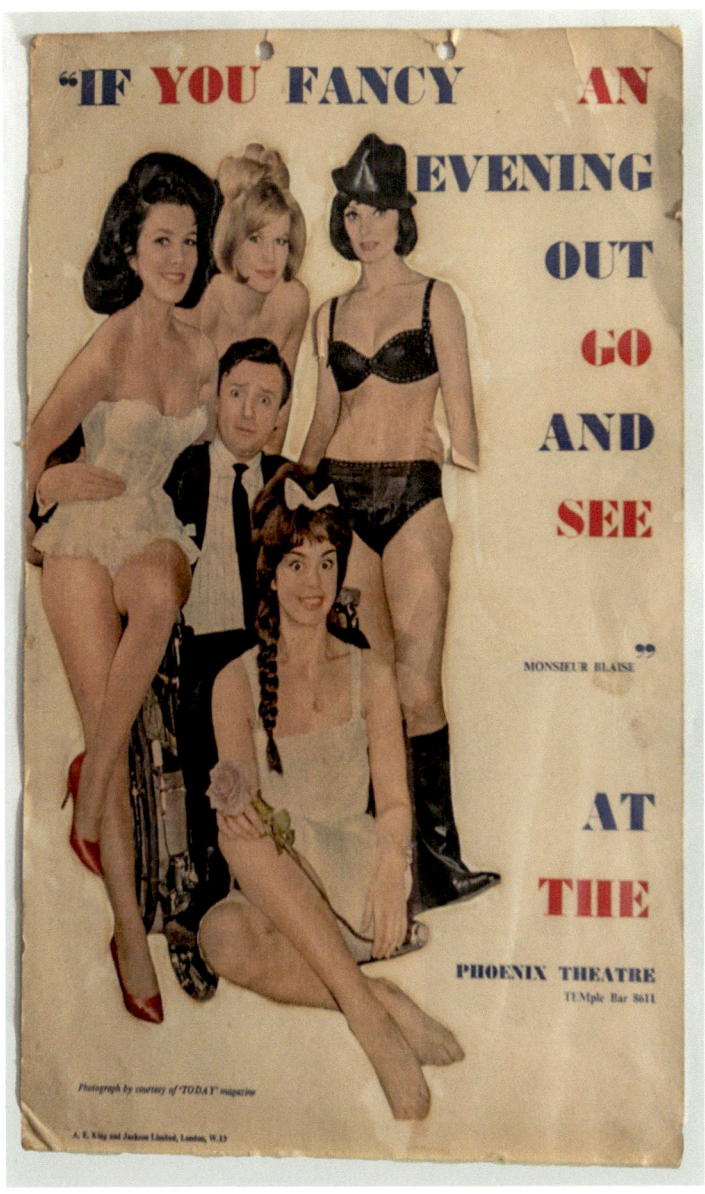

Monsieur Blaise. *This ran for six months. Jill spoke entirely in Spanish.*

Monsieur Blaise. *End of show cast party at the Phoenix Theatre.*

Tit-Bits *cover.*

Juke Box Jury. *David Jacobs and Jill. Part of the panel, judging the best and latest pop songs.*

The Morecambe and Wise film, The Magnificent Two.

Morecambe and Wise (and Jill). Eric playing the mad artist about to paint the naked lady.

Dave Prowse and Jill. Advert for the Bullworker.

Portrait.

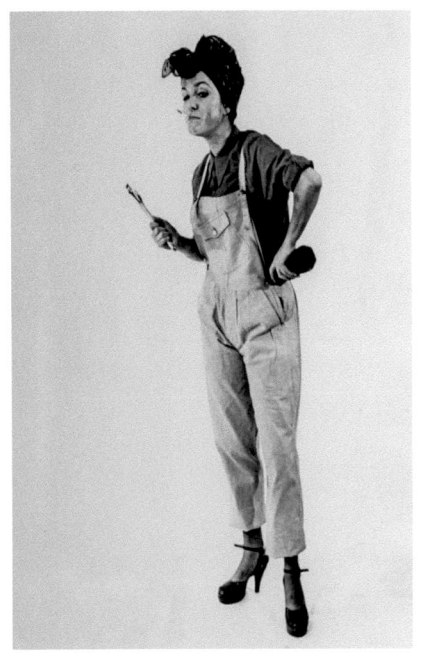

Wartime BBC sketch comedy.

Hugh and I. *Teaching Hugh how to do the Twist.*

Hugh and I *Christmas pageant.*

80,000 Suspects *with Claire Bloom and Director Val Guest.*

Walt Disney, with Eric Flynn in Dr. Synn.

Croquet in Pinewood.
Dr. Synn *lunch break.*

Bernard Cribbins, Peter Cushing and Jill.

Andrew Keir and Jill.

Jill and a Dalek. A publicity shot.

Miss World. Judging the contest at London Airport.

Jackie Stewart. Winning the clay pigeon shooting Olympic Trench Competition, North Wales Gun Club.

David Kosoff, Roger Moore and Jill at a charity event.

Jill shooting clays on the Olympic Trench layout at the North Wales Gun Club.

Mrs Baird's Bread, Texas. Taken at the Railroad Depot.

My ceramics.

Some of the trophies Jo Wheater won in one month in the early 1960s.

Jill's Beverly Hills pool.

Acting in Roberta *with Bob Hope, Dallas.*

Beverly Hills Century Plaza Hotel Moms and Moppets Fashion Parade, March, 1973.

The Doctor Who *family.*

CHAPTER THIRTEEN
DALEKS' INVASION EARTH 2150 AD

ONE OF the memorable things about Christmas 1965 was a phone call from my agent, Jean Drysdale. There'd been some enquiries made about me appearing in a sequel to *Doctor Who and the Daleks*, a film that had been a big hit during the summer. The producers clearly knew there was a demand for more, and the production was being prepared to start as soon as possible in the new year. Right from the start, you had a feeling that they were racing to get the whole thing ready. There was a definite and palpable sense of excitement about it.

For me, the world of sci-fi was all new. I was always quite busy with work commitments and never really had the chance to watch TV *Doctor Who*. Of course, I was more than aware of it and the cultural impact it was having on British children, but it just hadn't crossed my radar. I do remember the Daleks always being in the press, so I knew this was going to be something special.

Pretty soon after the call, I met with the producer Milton Subotsky and the director Gordon Flemyng, who was back again after making a success of the first movie. Peter Cushing would be returning as Dr Who, with Roberta

Tovey as his granddaughter Susan. Peter had previously worked with Milton on *Dr Terror's House of Horror* and *The Skull*. Alongside this, Bernard Cribbins was thrown into the mix. He'd recently completed *She* with Peter for Hammer Films.

Both Milton and Gordon outlined their plan to make Louise, my character, a strong role model for women. They wanted my costume to reflect that. My outfit was way ahead of its time. This was, of course, the general idea of the wardrobe supervisor, Jackie Cummins. There was a definite hint that Louise had been to the future. I wore tweed culottes and a very Sherlock Holmes-style jacket, which had wide Inverness cape-style sleeves. I also sported a beautiful pair of yellow suede boots, each of which featured two front zippers. I kept the boots for many years, but as one does in moments of madness, I eventually got rid of them. It was a foolish thing to do, as I am sure that they would have fetched much money on eBay

Of course, there was a read through at Shepperton studios. This broke the ice and everyone got to chat and say hello to one another, avoiding awkwardness on set.

But back to the Daleks!

I can be very specific about the first time I met one. It was on January 19th, for a photo call, where I dressed in a variety of crazy futuristic outfits, including a white bikini covered with black polka-dots. Nobody was inside operating the Daleks yet, so I had to lift their pincer arm and gun stick myself, to try and make them look a bit more animated.

Filming began on January 31st, 1966. I remember arriving at Shepperton Studios on my beloved Vespa, which until then I had mainly used for whizzing around the streets of swinging London. I was given a tour of the sets that were nearing completion on the sound stages, and it was then that the enormity of what I had signed up for started to dawn on me. The film sets were huge and had been wonderfully constructed by a great team of designers. I can remember seeing the full-scale lower section of the Dalek spacecraft and then the interiors for the first time and just thinking, *Wow!*

This amazing flying saucer stretched right across Stage H, complete with landing legs and a ramp leading inside, and it seemed like a whole street of incredibly authentic derelict buildings had been built around it. However, I was intrigued as to how it would look on screen. You see, the top half of the ship simply wasn't there. Gordon had the answer: a matte painting on glass had been prepared, the camera was pointed through this, and voilà, the illusion was complete.

Some of the first scenes I filmed were inside the TARDIS, as Bernard's policeman character, Tom, crashes through the doors and passes out. The room was full of fantastical equipment. It was slightly odd to film the first and last scenes of the film before anything else, but that was what the script dictated!

Peter Cushing was an absolute delight to work with – a very generous soul and a kind man. It came out later that during filming he hadn't been very well, but he soldiered on and gave his performance one hundred and ten percent. He always came prepared and rarely had to check his script as he had an almost photographic memory. Peter was the epitome of professionalism and wonderful company.

Peter and Roberta Tovey had previously worked together on the first film, so they got on very well. Peter was a like a real-life grandfather figure to Roberta, and he looked after her on set. It was such a lovely relationship the two of them had.

I think it was during the next stage of filming that the first bad accident took place. There's a long sequence in the film where rebel prisoners try and escape from the Daleks outside their spaceship. One of them runs across some gantry and up onto a wall, which leads across the derelict houses and onto a shop awning. The idea was for the Daleks to shoot him, and to see him fall onto some rubble below. They certainly rehearsed it and everything was fine, but when they came to actually shooting a take? Oh, boy!

Now, Eddie Powell, who was doing the stunt, was a pure professional. He was famously Christopher Lee's stunt double on many occasions, and I believe he had just played the Mummy for Hammer Films. He apparently tripped too soon on the top of the set, and fell onto the rubble badly, instantly breaking his ankle. But he was a trooper and, in spite of the pain, dragged himself down onto the ground to complete the take and get killed by the Daleks. He was whisked off in an ambulance, and was back before you knew it, his leg in plaster, so Gordon could get a shot of him lying dead on the ground to finish the sequence. That wasn't the end for Eddie, though. He hobbled around on crutches for the rest of filming, choreographing fight scenes as though there was nothing wrong.

I've often been asked about Peter getting ill while we were filming. I promise you, we weren't really aware that anything was badly wrong. I know it did get to the point that we had an unexpected couple of days off, but one assumed the sets were still being built or something like that. It was only later that I became aware that Milton had been forced to shut things down, and was able to claim quite a lot of money in insurance to cover the costs involved. Really, making a film is like being on a railway train. It's incredibly difficult to stop before you reach the final destination.

Bernard Cribbins was such fun to work with, and I recall it being difficult not to laugh during the conveyor belt sequence by the food machine. He was frantically trying to catch these paper plates being fired out loaded with sweets, before throwing them into a waste chute. The special effects team had a vacuum rigged up just behind that, and let me promise you, those plates really were being dragged in, without any acting being involved. Bernard was actually quite a quiet man, who always cycled to work on his beloved bike, as he didn't live that far from the studio. He always had his fishing tackle with him, quickly disappearing at lunchtime to see if he could catch anything for his tea.

I recall filming with Bernard the moment we had to jump out of the Dalek spaceship. It was quite a drop. I realised I couldn't land or roll properly with Louise's futuristic boots on, so it was so reassuring to know that Bernard was there to catch me. I trusted that he would, and he didn't let me down.

I think most of my scenes were with the lovely Ray Brooks and Andrew Keir, who had a wonderfully dry sense of humour, and Godfrey Quigley, who spent all of his time in a wheelchair as Dortmun. I know Andrew hurt his hand badly when they were filming him smashing his fist through the window of a van.

The other incident, of course, was the day the Dalek caught fire.

I remember there was a bit of a ruckus with Robert Jewell, who had a heavy Australian accent that you could clearly hear coming out of his Dalek. Occasionally you would hear him swearing when he bumped into things during rehearsals. Anyway, he got together with Gordon, and there was an agreement reached that he could train new Dalek operators for the second film. So the normal guys, who were also BBC Daleks, got short shrift and lost out on movie number two. As a result, they were angry with Robert. If the Daleks had been in a union, we'd have been in trouble.

So, yes, the burning Dalek.

As far as I recall, it was during the riot where the rebels try to escape from the flying saucer. The rebels were supposed to push one of the Daleks down the ramp leading inside. It was meant to crash, and a pyrotechnic charge should have gone off with a bit of smoke to show it had been killed. Something went wrong, and the charge exploded like a bomb. Smoke was streaming everywhere, and we all rushed in to try and help the poor man inside to get out. There was a bit of a panic that he had breathed in too much smoke, but thankfully after a few minutes he was fine. However dangerous it was, it did give Gordon quite a spectacular shot in the finished movie.

The opening sequences, where the TARDIS arrives in the future, were shot on Stage H. The set was enormous, and you felt that the ambition Gordon had was being realised, although he could get quite agitated and frustrated. I think he was always pushing himself to get that extra shot. Even today, many people think that Dr Who and his friends exploring the decimated buildings by the River Thames was shot on location, but it wasn't. The only thing that was done for real is when the Dalek rises out of the water. The film was mostly filmed indoors, thanks to the wonderful sets and crew.

I found the press interest in me increased greatly during filming. It was like becoming the science fiction version of a Bond girl! The *Evening Standard* even ran a piece about me getting caught in traffic jams, and being late in getting to the studio, while the *Eastern Evening News* ran an interview with me with the wonderful headline, 'The Daleks Are Darlings, Aren't They?'. Journalists were different then. You almost got to know them, and there were so many magazines and film gossip columns. I know that *Titbits* ran a piece on me making the Dalek movie, and yes that was its real name!

My last bit of filming was, as far as I recall, in Battersea, down by the River Thames, where Louise gets a wet handkerchief for Susan's injuries. It's actually one of the earliest scenes in the film. The filming seemed to rush by so quickly, and the finished film was out at the cinemas in a matter of months. We finished mid-March, and it was released late July. The budget was £286,000, and I'm told that's double what Milton spent on the first film. However, he was a shrewd businessman. If you look closely, you'll see discreet adverts peppered around derelict London for Sugar Puffs, the breakfast cereal, and the manufacturers paid £50,000 for the pleasure!

In recent years, I have attended quite a few conventions and met many wonderful fans of the Dalek films. It's always heart-warming to hear how this film impacted on people's lives when they were growing up. It's also lovely to meet a new generation of young fans who are discovering the Dalek movies for the first time. The question I always seem to get asked is, 'What was it like working with the Daleks?' I am always happy to respond positively. 'They were an absolute joy!'

I am very fond of my role in *Daleks' Invasion Earth 2150 AD*. It was a combination of real swashbuckling action, vast sets and genuine excitement – a flash-bang experience that I really didn't understand at the time. I had no idea of how important it would prove in cinematic sci-fi history for almost sixty years and counting. *Daleks' Invasion Earth 2150 AD* was billed as 'Today's Fantastic Adventure', and this billing is still the perfect description.

CHAPTER FOURTEEN
HOLLYWOOD AND SUNSET BOULEVARD

IN 1967 work opportunities were becoming fewer. Added to this, Nicky and I had gone our separate ways. With wistfulness, I recall sitting in my Maida Vale flat. It was an overcast day and I was looking inwards rather than outwards. Uppermost in my thoughts was the need to move on. Surely the grass was greener elsewhere.

It felt like everything that I had enjoyed now gave me a feeling of claustrophobia. My inner voice was imploring me to find my wings. Derek was now living in Hollywood, so why not me too? Here was an opportunity, and if I did not take it I never would.

I quickly made plans and gathered up all that was important to me. My belongings included two pieces of 'I must have forever' furniture. I couldn't bear to be parted from my Danish teak desk and bookcase. This priceless furniture was taken to the Pan Am shipping offices. I then carefully packed up everything else I wanted to take, ready for the flight to Los Angeles.

My savings didn't amount to much. But I had just enough to purchase my Pan Am 121 tickets to begin my new life starting January 25th, 1968. It was an enjoyable flight, especially as I joined Terry Thomas, who had a spare seat next to him in first class. We drank champagne he had smuggled onto the plane, toasting each other's health and good fortune.

Having crossed the Atlantic, we flew over the Rockies, a brown and white patchwork quilt far below. Refuelling at Montreal, the stopover was so quick that we were unable to stretch our legs, but I did get the chance to chat with the Yugoslavian actor Chase Cordell.

Arriving in Los Angeles, I was met by Derek. My ex had arranged the rental of a small flat opposite his own, situated on Fountain Avenue in Hollywood. Derek again rigged up a wire that connected his flat with mine. Amusingly, the wire traversed the car park below. As in our London apartments, we were able to use walkie-talkies to save tying up our more important telephone lines. Once again, I had my little place on God's earth. I was newly independent with a little added security. This was my new world and everything of course was unfamiliar to me.

Now I had the hard work of breaking into the Hollywood film industry. Thankfully I had an impressive track record and my curriculum vitae had bells on it. But here in Hollywood I was admittedly an unknown actress and one of a great many aspiring personalities. I was, in fact, making a fresh start and doing so in the toughest town of all. Here there was no shortage of actors and actresses and most with impressive portfolios.

Of course, I had my history of theatre, television and movie roles with me. With my CV in my bag, I hit the ground running, but alas offers from agents were as rare as hen's teeth. Agents are essential links between artiste and producer; in fact, there are few engagements made directly with individuals in the film world.

From day one I set about visiting every agent listed or who had been recommended. Time after time I traipsed up and down Sunset Boulevard knocking on closed doors, and time after time I returned empty-handed.

Derek had been more fortunate and had signed up with the Lew Sherrill agency. I met Lew too and found him to be very nice and kind, but unable to see where my acting abilities might fit in. I felt like I had hit a brick wall. Meanwhile, Derek was paying a fee to a very well-regarded public relations company. Russell Birdwell had a reputation for turning newcomers into stars. So, having what he thought an excellent start with his English background and considerable experience, my ex-husband shelled out $2,000, which was a considerable sum of money. This outlay was offset by his confidence. My former husband was absolutely certain he would soon see his name in lights. Sure, it might take a month or so but he had patience.

Arriving together, I was well-received and hit it off immediately with Russell Birdwell. He seemed to know more than any other about the ins and outs of the industry. I found him kind, witty and very understanding. I tried to explain the difficulties to Derek, but my ex never really understood the PR and studio way of doing business. It is a fallacy to think that it has much in common with other commercial concerns as it does not. Besides, luck plays a very big part in things too – the right place, time and desk, all that sort of thing. Russell had just written a book called *Women in Battle Dress* and he gave me a copy which he inscribed, 'Jill Curzon, who wears so beautifully the battle dress of the 20th century. Welcome to America.'

I arrived in the US in January 1968, and during that first month, I was to meet many people. One important contact was Bob Christianson, the editor of *The Hollywood Reporter*, whose offices were found on Sunset Boulevard. His periodical was the weekly bible of the show business industry. Leafing through its pages you discovered everything you really needed to know about the show business side of things. A very important feature was news of the upcoming auditions and casting of films taking place at the industry's many studios. The periodical's rival was *Variety*, which had many similarities but went into finer detail and especially so in live entertainment.

Bob took me to lunch at Cyrano's, which was the usual place for the show business set to have lunch. Likewise, there was also The Brown Derby, where you would commonly see Hedder Hoppa and Louella Parsons, the two most important columnists in town. These rivals achieved fame or notoriety for their gritty exposure of the scandals, gossip and rumours then circulating. My table companion was very impressed with my CV and from then on encouraged me a great deal.

Things were now happening with breathtaking speed. On February 3rd, 1968, Derek and I dashed to the airport, from where we took a flight to Las Vegas. Upon our arrival, we went to the county court and re-married. There was little choice, because it was the only way I was going to get the essential green card, the working and residence permit of the United States.

Derek held dual nationality status due to his having an American mother and an English father. The re-marriage caused me great upset, but circumstances left me no choice but to go through with this sham wedding. I had to put dark glasses on in an effort to disguise my emotions. Derek even forgot to pay the $43 for the licence; it was the best theatre I had ever played. Needless to say the marriage was annulled very shortly afterwards. After a quick drink at the airport, not to toast but to settle my nerves, we caught the plane back to Los Angeles.

Chase was waiting to pick up the newly wedded bride and we went to a party organised by Tim and Janet Brown. Terry Thomas telephoned the next day and he wanted to discuss a possible part. Later, Chase gave me a lift to the Beverley Hills Hotel. There we had dinner with Rita and Norman Hudis. I knew Norman was the writer of *The Man from Uncle*, the lead parts of which were played by Robert

Vaughn and David McCallum, so we had much to talk about.

Sylvain Zait was a recommended French photographer. He took several pictures of me, all of which were black-and-white. This seemed to add to the appeal of the photographs. In the meantime, I had a script that Derek had picked up for me to consider. The work was by Sonny Bono of the Sonny and Cher duo, a film called *Chastity*.

After thoroughly familiarising myself with the script I acted the part opposite Mike Arciega with Sonny and the director, Alessio de Pada. I thought it all went well, but on reflection I reminded myself that I must detach myself. And what better way than with a glass of wine at Cyrano's?

This period was filled with promise but little else. The interviews were coming in at a regular pace. I was supported by Bob Christenson, Russell Birdwell, Norman Hudis, and Terry Thomas, just some of the great friendships I was able to make. But of all these opportunities, nothing seemed to stick.

Networking among the young and the ambitious is commonplace and a very good strategy for quickly getting into the right lane for the right contacts. Things were a little different then, as such interacting was done at social occasions arranged for the purpose of pressing the right flesh. I suppose it was like going to the employment bureau and was all part of life's rich tapestry.

Like London, it was the nightspots that drew the right faces. There was The Playboy Club, 604 and The Factory. Oh, and The Daisy, where I had met Donald Sutherland and his wife Shirley. I was again in the couple's company at a party arranged to fete Janet Suzman's birthday.

In Los Angeles, I had interviews with NBC, where I met Rowan and Martin of *Laugh-In*. There also was Judy Carne, whom I knew from my life in London, where John Kennedy had been her manager. I recall receiving a nice letter from my London agent Gerry Maxin that cheered me up a great deal. It was nice to know that he remembered me. He was very supportive and went to great lengths to encourage me.

I also received a call from Gordon Flemyng, my director friend from the Dalek movie. Having arrived in Los Angeles, he was keen to help me and we were to meet on several occasions. He'd become a name in Hollywood after completing a Peter O'Toole movie called *The Great Catherine*, and was preparing a gangster thriller called *The Split*, but sadly any talk of me appearing in it didn't work out.

By the middle of February, I had met Herbert Leonard, who was the producer of *Naked City*. He later called me and said he would like me to read a part in his script called *Popi*. If the project left the ground my co-star would be Alan Arkin. I was driven down to Bert Leonard's home on Malibu beach. There we had a very enjoyable Hawaiian lunch and during the following two hours we spent time examining the script.

At the end of our study, I offered two suggestions that interested him and was invited to return home with the script to give it further thought. The part that was set for me was that of Lupe, a Cuban girl.

Everything seemed to be perfectly above board and there was complete transparency about the well thought out project. This made a refreshing change from being fed false promises, some of which I had admittedly fed myself.

Derek, in the meantime, was busy with his new Perazzi shotgun and furthering his interest in shooting. Meanwhile, I would often visit Norman and Rita Hudis and admire the former's new 1965 Thunderbird Chevrolet. It was a super car; I enjoyed sharing the ride with him when we would go to the store. During one excursion, my good friend unburdened himself and I learned that he was having a tough time with Rita. I felt so sorry for him, as he was an easy-going guy and what you saw was what you got. Rita was a nurse and did not like the USA; eventually they went back to the UK and then settled in Ireland.

Following more photo sessions with Silvain, we drove to the MGM Studios to drop the pictures on the desks of the King brothers. While there, we enjoyed a few drinks in what was known as the re-take room. On the set, we could see Donald Sutherland, and we had lunch with Gordon Flemyng. Rock Hudson was filming with Julie Andrews.

The Reporter ran a piece on Derek and I, and this was brought to us by Bob Christensen. This event was also followed by Ralph Story, who was completing a five-minute piece on KNX Radio regarding Derek and me. This broadcast apparently went down very well.

'Perhaps you would like to come to New York with me,' Bert Leonard said with a smile. 'You will meet the movie director Arthur Hiller and the cast is at his suite in the Warwick Hotel.'

I laboured for a full 1.5 seconds to make a decision – we only live once! On March 1st, 1968, accompanied by Bert Leonard, I flew to New York, hoping to secure the part of Lupe in *Popi*.

Soon after we landed in New York, we were joined for drinks by John King. A good friend of Bert's, he was staying in the next-door suite. Being there on a business trip, Bert had invited John to join his pre-film cast party. I, of course, didn't know John, but was soon to learn that he was the vice-president of McCulloch Oil of California.

John was accompanied by Eva Sutter and we chatted amiably. I thought John a little quiet and withdrawn for a 'broad Stetson hat oil man'.

During our New York visit, Bert took me to see many of the Big Apple's interesting places, and I became acquainted with many fascinating people. Going to the Biltmore Theatre was both interesting and fun. We enjoyed seeing *The Staircase* and afterwards met Eli Wallach and Milo O'Shea. In the case of the latter, we recalled the drama in which we had played the main parts, ITV's Play of the Week *Mrs Quilley's Murder Shoes*.

Then I was off to see Mildred, who was the cousin of Derek's mother, Louise. As one might expect she was waiting for us in a classic English tea setting, and later we went up the Empire State Building. Being such a clear crisp day, it was the perfect time and place to take in the Manhattan panorama at forty-eight floors up.

While in New York, I was interviewed by Marion Doherty, a casting director. There was perhaps a part for me in a Czech film to be started in July.

Back in Hollywood I had a nasty shock when a well-known producer stormed in my apartment without a word, exposing his manliness. Taken aback, I told him to leave immediately, after which I never set eyes on him again. Unfortunately, Derek had found us our apartments in the seedier side of Hollywood instead of the more upmarket Beverly Hills, but he did not know any better at the time.

About six months later, I was on one of my regular visits to Universal Studios to attend a meeting with the casting directors. I was following up job opportunity printouts published in *The Hollywood Reporter*. Following the meeting, I headed for the lot where I had parked my car. As I was delving into my bag for the token to open the barrier, I was approached by a stocky little man running across towards me.

'Stop, don't put your token in, come with me!'

The guy was none other than Lew Sherrell. You don't say no to an approach like that, so I followed him up to the office of the movie director Joe Sargeant. There, I was given to read the part of an English secretary; finding a suitable actress had so far proved elusive. Casting the part was time sensitive as the shooting was to begin in just two days. When I left the two men, I was walking on air. I had the part. Now there were only the lines to learn. I was in!

CHAPTER FIFTEEN
JOHN KING AND McCULLOCH OIL

I DATED John King on a couple of occasions and I now needed his help. As it happened, it was a requirement to be a paid-up member of the Screen Actors Guild before I could even go near a film set. Problem: I simply didn't have the $200 membership fee.

I discussed my dilemma with John, who agreed to help me out, and he arranged to meet me at the Guild's office on Sunset Boulevard. Despite leaving his office in good time, the traffic was so heavy that he couldn't make the 5pm closing time. Vainly, I stood on the office steps with the contract in my hand while looking for his large black Lincoln Continental saloon. Desperate, I pleaded with the girl at the desk to wait just a moment, telling her my friend was on his way. She kindly did so, and John finally pulled up outside. It was 5.10pm and, moments later, I picked up my SAG card.

The following day saw me on Universal Studio's sound stage ready to play my first Hollywood part. The film, *The Sunshine Patriot*, was directed by Joseph Sargent. It also starred Cliff Robertson and his wife Dina Merrill. It was a good part. It was not too small and was an excellent cameo.

My scenes mainly involved working alongside the wonderfully eccentric Wilfred Hyde White, who was more concerned with who'd won the latest race at Aintree rather than remembering his lines, but his sheer charm helped him get away with it.

I was finally acting in Hollywood and it felt wonderful! All the sad months of fruitless toil evaporated and became meaningless. But Lew Sherrell still hadn't signed me up, and there was another similar part to follow. This would also take place at Universal Studios, and again I was cast as a secretary to my boss, the Colonel, played by John Williams. *It Takes a Thief* starred Robert Wagner. He played Alexander Mundy, who was a rather sophisticated cat burglar, who the US Government used on top secret jobs. My scenes were mainly with Robert and there was one particular scene that was unforgettable.

Robert Wagner was playing the part of an English army officer, as Mundy was in disguise for one of his missions. His part required him to talk while he was descending a long spiral staircase. The scene had to be retaken several times because in the middle of the discourse he had to say the word 'lieutenant'. As an English army officer, the word would be pronounced 'leftenant' but my co-star kept on using the American pronunciation, 'lootenant'. In the end, he gave up and the entire scene went on to the cutting room floor – that's show business!

Around about this time, John had left his wife Laverne. She hadn't taken the separation lightly and soon discovered where we were living. One night she paid us a call and sugar was furtively poured into the fuel tank of my Triumph TR2. My engine was ruined and John felt obliged to replace my car.

Also at this point in time, Bob McCulloch and CV Wood went to London to purchase London Bridge. The rumour was that the two had confused London Bridge with Tower Bridge, but this was not actually the case. Soon every granite of stone was numbered, dismantled, and then shipped to Lake Havasu City in Arizona. The geography was modified to accommodate the bridge in its new home. However, there were too many stones for the planned crossing, so the excess stones were cut and sold as souvenirs in Harrods department store.

October 9th 1971 was the opening of the relocated London Bridge and John and I were invited. What a celebration it was! There was a festive dinner on the bridge, attended by many guests wearing period dress. I appeared as Nell Gwynn. There were fireworks galore, speeches, and the Lord Mayor of London Sir Peter Studd arrived by barge amid a great fanfare with white doves released and fireworks wowing the crowds. Accompanying the mayor was Dick Tomkins, of The Honourable Artillery Company, who knew my father. Best English ale was consumed at a typical English pub, and a London double decker bus resided outside.

A year earlier, in June 1970, Robert McCulloch Senior retired as president of McCulloch Oil. At this point, John as vice-president presumed he would step into the position and would become the company's president. However, the position went instead to the retiring president's son, Robert McCulloch Jr.

Dismayed, John accepted an offer of vice-presidency of the Amarex Oil Company, the president being Jim Templeton. This meant we had to move from Los Angeles to Oklahoma City. In Oklahoma City I acquired Muffin, my pedigree Yorkshire terrier. John was busy working downtown and I felt lonely. Muffin was lovely and we walked in the garden complex a lot.

I landed an acting role at Oklahoma Television and played the part of the wicked witch in a children's programme. This, I remember, was great fun. The programme had no script and each episode we ad-libbed. Seat of your pants stuff!

Later, down in Texas, I became involved with the theatre. I was asked to take part in a Bob Hope musical to celebrate his wedding anniversary with Dolores. One member of the cast was Jamie Farr from *M*A*S*H*, one of the best TV series ever made in America in my humble opinion. It was great fun. We had three performances, and after each one the actors were invited to have dinner at the houses of oil barons, one of whom was Clint Murchison Jr, who started the Dallas Cowboys football team.

We also visited Fort Worth with an old friend Ed Van Zandt, who had written a book called *The Iron Orchard* about a typical oil career, blended with social satire. They were planning to make a film version, and he wanted me to play the wife in it. This would have been very exciting, but unfortunately the film never happened.

Sadly, John didn't settle well into Amarex Oil and was very unhappy. We had a few happy times including a trip to Las Vegas, where I became pregnant and John won $4,800. He was a good craps player. Thankfully I managed to stop him playing before losing his winnings and this enabled us to buy our furniture.

Events moved on, and John and his friend, Buddy Williams, negotiated a deal to transport LNG (Liquified Natural gas) and LPG (Liquified Petroleum gas) from Houston to McCulloch Oil in California. We leased two trucks, one Mack, the other a Fruehauf. The company was called The Wyoming Transport & Trading Company. I managed the finances and taxes for the company. This initiative brought us in a very nice $9000 a month, so we could easily pay our monthly rent of $1,700 for our new home at 9963 Beverly Grove Drive, Beverly Hills, California in August 11th 1971. Our next-door neighbour were Sandy and Don O'Neill, the other side being Cary Grant.

We also bought two cars tax free in Oregon. Mine was a white Cadillac Fleetwood Brougham. John bought himself a tan-coloured Cadillac Eldorado. We were now financially very comfortable, and our home was the sort of impressive residence that features on the best glossy magazine covers. We had a prize-winning designer swimming pool, which was beautiful, and a great view over Los Angeles.

Michelle Claudia King was born on February 26th 1972 at St John's Hospital in Santa Monica. It was a private room that Liz Taylor had used when she had had her babies. Being Rhesus Negative, I had my blood type standing by in case Michelle was born a blue baby and needed immediate transfusion. The birth was induced and I had an epidural, which meant I could watch it all on a TV placed at the end of the bed. I had no pain and Michelle was perfect and it was a wonderful experience. John and I married on June 23rd 1972 in Las Vegas.

I had become active member of the community. I joined the American National Theatre Association (ANTA), the president of which was John Forsyth of *Dynasty* Fame. Soon afterwards I was elected to the board of the ladies' section, ANTANS.

John Bloom, of washing machine fame in England, arrived, and upon his being permitted residency, he rented the home of the novelist Harold Robbins. Bloom approached ANTANS to request that his wife have a place on the board, but because she was new and inexperienced she failed to impress. This irritated John Bloom, and afterwards he telephoned criticising me for voting against her. We all felt she was too new and should have some more experience first.

Ours was a formidable association that, due to my inspiration, had the clout to charter an Intercontinental Navigation airliner to transport American Shakespeare fans to the English bard's Stratford-upon-Avon place of birth, which was very successful.

I was also involved in various charitable organisations and used my skills to arrange events. These were mostly fundraising dinners at the Beverly Wilshire and Beverly Hill's hotels. These events raised considerable funds that were to benefit many good causes. It was at one of the committee meetings that I became acquainted with the legendary Martha Scott and Jane Russell of WAIF, who was so lovely and charming – we got on so well. And then I belonged to PHP. – 'People Helping People' – and also the 'Impossibles', which was all ladies off course. We had a lot of fun.

Another notable associate was Jimmy Doolittle, the impresario who was responsible for bringing the Royal Ballet to California. I was honoured to be invited by Jimmy to join him for lunch with the administrative director, Anthony Russell-Roberts of London's Royal Ballet. It so happened that he and his wife went on holiday with Nicky Henson and his ballerina wife. Doolittle was an excellent organiser and we enjoyed going to his house parties. He also organised the re-opening of the Greek Theatre with the ANTANS, and performer Alice Cooper.

Another neighbourhood friend was C V Wood (CEO of McCulloch Oil Co). It was in his house, the bedroom to be precise, that we watched Neil Armstrong become the first man on the moon on July 21st 1969.

CHAPTER SIXTEEN
BYE BYE BEVERLY HILLS

ONE NICE thing happened in March 1973. Michelle and I were invited to *The Mom's and Moppets Show*, a charity fashion extravaganza at the Century Plaza Hotel. Michelle was walking at ten months old, so she managed the catwalk very well. There were other actresses and moppets and it was wonderful fun.

Then Wyoming Transport & Trading ended, which was no surprise. It was great while it lasted, but I always knew that we needed to think ahead, so what would be our next move?

We moved back to Houston, the hub of oil deals in America. We chose a small townhouse in Town & Country Estates, just outside the main city. John was busy contacting everyone he knew as we had a little reserve of money, but it would not last very long.

This was when we met the Lees, a lovely English family and our next-door neighbours. Roland Lees was the financial director of the Royal Dutch Shell company. Michelle was one and a half by then, and their little girls were a bit older, but they enjoyed playing together at the swimming pool.

One day, John was off to Lexington, Kentucky and I really wanted to go too, having heard a lot about this place.

Luckily, Muriel, Roland's wife, said she would look after Michelle, and we went for two days.

When we returned, a troubled Muriel told us that there had been an accident in the supermarket. Apparently an aquarium had fallen off a shelf and hit Michelle on the head. She was rushed to hospital, but it was only a slight cut and graze. But poor Muriel was really upset. To be fair, it was not Muriel's fault, but one of the staff who had left the aquarium too near the edge. It all ended OK, thank God!

Then, in the summer, my dad came to visit us from East Horsley. It was great, but the summers in Houston are not so pleasant. They are very hot and humid, and every day at 5pm, there is a thunderstorm and very heavy rain. This lasts for about half an hour, then the heat starts to steam and it is hot and sticky again.

The other big drama involved Dad, Michelle, Muriel's little girls and me. This involved a supermarket nearby. It suddenly went very dark in the mid-afternoon and then there was a strange rumbling noise outside.

I thought, *Oh no, another thunderstorm.*

The noise got louder and louder and we were all slightly scared, and then the lights in the market went off, and we saw this great black funnel in the air coming towards us – it was a tornado!

Well, what do we do?

I telephoned John asking him to drive over and rescue us. He jumped into his car in his dressing gown. On the way, there was a huge crash; the roof of the nearby cinema came flying over him and into the roof of the supermarket. Everyone was panicking except John. He arrived with no windows in the car and his head and hair covered in shattered glass. I don't think he would have ventured out of the house had he not been drinking. Everyone scattered and ran to their cars and jumped in and, by this time, the tornado had passed through and gone on to wreak more havoc.

After a very few months, John got lucky and accepted a job as vice president of Ascot Oil in Shreveport, Louisiana, the company owned by James Cunningham. This was very exciting for Michelle and me. We found this lovely house to rent at 9401 Red Oak Lane. We had great neighbours and made friends with most on the street. This part of the south is wonderful. The few short years there were mostly good for me, but not for John.

CHAPTER SEVENTEEN
SHEREVEPORT

WE LIVED in Shreveport, Louisiana between 1974 and 1976. Our new home backed on to the Shreveport East Ridge Country Club and I decided to take up golf lessons. I did so with the thought that John might also show an interest, but this was not to be. My dear husband could think only of business and football. For my part, I watched football on TV with him. I actually enjoyed American football and I learned much about the game. One supposes I had adopted the strategy, 'If you can't beat them then join them.'

We made good friends in Shreveport including Bob McIntyre's wife, Wanda, who lived further down our road. We enjoyed attending ceramic classes together, where I made some lovely gumbo bowls. These were then painted, glazed, and then popped into the kiln. I recall, in particular, a commemorative ashtray, which bore the words, '1976 – 200th Anniversary of the United States'. Yes, there was a big bicentenary to be celebrated in 1976, and no one parties like the Americans and especially the southerners.

Later on, I shipped this pottery back to Europe where it ended up in Dad's garage in East Horsley. By 1980, his garage was a storeroom for so many boxes and for much of my travelling furniture too. This meant that his car had to stay in the driveway come rain or shine. He was so sweet about it, and never once complained, though he did mention that through the cold winters the points of the local railway tracks were frozen, and so were his car windows.

During our time in Shreveport, Dad visited us twice. He loved everything about our home and the neighbourhood. Everything was so removed from typical England. Of course, we wined and dined, and it really was such fun to be with him. He enjoyed the southern tradition of horse racing and he placed a few bets at Louisiana Downs.

While he was there, the annual dance was held at the East Ridge Country Club. This was where things got interesting. Wanda knew a lady whom she thought might like to accompany Dad. He was reluctant to be paired off and he took much persuading, but Wanda assured us she was a lovely woman.

Well, this lady friend turned up at our home dressed head-to-toe in a leopard outfit. To describe the outfit as clinging would be an understatement. She also had a bush of red hair, offset by masses of inappropriate jewellery. It was all too much; her outfit was too awful that one couldn't even snicker or laugh – poor Dad. The initial shock did wear off, but just when you think things couldn't possibly get worse…

His new lady friend got my reluctant father onto the dance floor. This was never his thing at the best of times. Dad was a stiff upper lip British Army officer and the last person on earth I would expect to go with the flow and let his hair down, let alone with such a companion. It was difficult to imagine a more ill-suited couple. How we got through that evening I will never know, but like all things good and bad it had an ending. Not that Dad ever forgot the occasion.

Our home had three bedrooms, three bathrooms, a games room, a huge lounge and dining room, and wonderfully spacious kitchen. John and I had walk-in wardrobes. The bedrooms were spacious and, as one might expect, en-suite. The gardens were lined with pines. They almost formed a guard of honour away from the house and onto the seventeenth green of the golf club.

Michelle had a lovely play area that included a swing set. All in all, it was the loveliest home we had ever lived in. The price was quite reasonable at $70,000 paltry by today's standards. We were also blessed with good neighbours, and this is always a bonus.

When we had first arrived with our moving truck, our neighbours, Sid and Pat, were waiting to greet us with iced tea and hamburgers. It was such a wonderful southern welcome. Our new neighbours thoughtfully presumed that we had no food or beverages waiting for us in our new home.

Pat and I soon became lifelong friends. An energetic and talented woman, Pat loved to paint the homes of others in our neighbourhood. Her client base was impressive, including J. Paul Getty and other famous people. I was fortunate enough to purchase one of her paintings for just $120. This was an oil canvas of a basket of beautifully coloured zinnias and today the painting takes pride of place in our hallway in Marbella. It brings me great joy each time I pass it for in that bouquet of flowers is carried the most beautiful images and memories.

Pat had two daughters and a son, two of whom were music lovers, although both were a bit hippy, which at the time was all the style. Vicki, the eldest of Pat's daughters, often babysat for Michelle.

Sid worked in the insurance business. It was a steady job and it brought home the bacon but I thought it all sounded so boring. Pat was much more of a free spirit and also entrepreneurial. Sometime in the 1990s, Sid passed away. After she had recovered, Pat became very friendly – well in love actually – with the family dentist. His wife had died and had left him as widower. Theirs was a relationship that was heaven blessed and they were really happy together. The two have a great deal in common and perhaps more so than my friend had with her late husband.

CHAPTER EIGHTEEN
AN UNEXPECTED TELEPHONE CALL

As the end of January grew closer the weather remained bitterly cold. Then on the 17th the phone rang and a voice said, 'Is that Jill?'

I knew who the caller was, despite never actually hearing her speak. I instinctively knew it was Stefanie, my twenty-one-year-old daughter, who had been adopted at birth. At the time of Stefanie's birth, I was seventeen-years old.

Stefanie had tracked me down. I asked my long-lost daughter how she had found me. She told me it was through her birth certificate. The document had me down as Jill Shirley Planterose. It was quite easy for my daughter to scour the telephone directories and find my father, Howard Planterose of Surrey. A resourceful young woman, Stefanie had called him to explain that she was an old friend of mine. On asking for my telephone number, he obliged her.

To say you could have knocked me over with a feather would have been an understatement – her call literally blew my mind. After asking me if I was Jill, her next question was, 'Do you know who and where my father is?'

I told her that her father was John Boryer of Haywards Heath in Sussex. Later, she discovered that my ex-lover had since married and now had two children.

Two days later, she told her boss Mike Samson and he was delighted for her. She was now on a mission to see me and we were soon arranging her flights to Shreveport. Gladly, I sent my long-lost daughter $764 to cover her outlay for her anticipated seven to fourteen days she would stay with us.

It was Friday, January 28th when our eagerly awaited reunion was to take place. Hardly able to breathe, I climbed into our car and left for the airport.

As I saw my daughter, it truly felt like the earth stopped still. I could hardly think straight, let alone cope with my emotions. I recognised her immediately, and after hugging endlessly, we took the road home and spent the evening drinking champagne, eating and showering each other with recollections and compliments.

Our old life ended and our new life began and we retired to our beds well after 4am. I thanked her for bringing us together again. We cuddled and I suppose there were a few tears of gratitude shed, and I told her I loved her and how proud of her I was.

The next day was well into its stride when we awoke. Perhaps we should have stayed under our duvets. Outside, it was snowing hard and Michelle was happy to see the snow.

Later, I took Stefanie over to meet Pat and Sid. Both were by now in the picture and were sharing our joy. Then we were off to ERCC where we enjoyed a togetherness lunch and afterwards we took a stroll in the snow. It was a Christmas-card landscape, the sun showering us with blessings as our now larger family ambled along.

That evening, Stefanie and I had dinner out together and we danced at Sansones. Much more was to follow. There were shopping trips, lunches, walks and excited exchanges as we chatted about all those missing years. From the start, Stefanie enthusiastically embraced our way of life, part of which was accompanying us to Michelle's school to enjoy a show. John was meanwhile totally absorbed in sorting out job related issues with MCO, C V Wood and Mike Witte.

Stefanie wasn't one for allowing the grass to grow under her feet. My daughter met up with a guy she had talked with during our evening at Sansones. What followed was the pair's disappearance to Louisiana Downs horse racing events. Not that Stefanie's day ended there: my long-lost daughter got lost again. It was 3.30am when she returned, but she was happy to have arrived back home. Whatever the two were enjoying together, she felt sufficiently inspired to get together with him again.

Since Stefanie's arrival, we two had become addicted to watching the then dated TV show *The Little Rascals*. The series caused many bouts of laughing. Otherwise, it was all go.

John had a trip planned to go to LA and we decided to take Stefanie with us. We dropped Michelle off at Mrs Welsh's, who would look after her. We then packed and were soon ready early to join Roger and Harry Stetingal on the private Cessna jet to pick up Buddy Williams in Houston.

We flew to Los Angeles with pilots Pat and Chuck and inebriated Seldon Harris and onto the Marina Rey Club. There we stayed with Stefanie.

We swam to our hearts content, dined and wined and slept really well. Well, I say that but Stefanie was actually still at the bar.

It was necessary for me to have a quiet word with Stefanie, whose customary position at the bar was now similar to that of a truck driver. I had to explain protocol: that ladies did not drink alone at the bar; it was different from English pubs. Stefanie didn't take too kindly to my sermon. We exchanged words but we did make up afterwards. I heard later that she had been chatted up by Leigh Davis of the Davis Club set. My errant daughter certainly wasted no time in settling into her new but temporary lifestyle.

We were soon ready for our return flights. Stefanie, who had arranged to spend the day at the Redondo beach with a family she had met, was unable to join us. Without her, we made our way back to Shreveport, and Stefanie made her own way back.

She later called from Dallas to say she was fine. This was her first visit to the States and what a lot of ground she had covered in three weeks. It was also nice that Stefanie and Michelle got on so well.

Finally, Stefanie left for the UK via Chicago on March 11th. Overall, it had been a good visit but it had been filled with much drama, some of which was a little traumatic. It seemed to me that Stefanie felt some animosity towards me.

Years later, I discovered that she blamed me for, 'abandoning her at birth'. It took Stefanie many years to come to terms with the reality of my life in England in 1955. It was hard to explain my position to her. I was a sixteen-year-old studying hard for my GCE exams and then I had discovered I was pregnant. I think my parents handled things well enough, in keeping with the norms of the times. Then, unlike now, I had little or no control over my life from the time of Stefanie's birth. At least the aforementioned narrative gave me an excellent grounding in the rudiments of nursing. As far as Stefanie was concerned, the decisions were by far the best for her too. Throughout her childhood, my daughter was cherished by the most wonderful family one could hope for. She and I are very close now, which is great. And she is happily married and lives in France, after selling her large kennels and cattery facilities in Estepona, Spain.

*

John was drinking heavily now. He was very unhappy and his health wasn't good. This was something that concerned me greatly, particularly when he began to experience abdominal pain. John had gall stones, a serious condition that was further aggravated by his suffering a badly ulcerated stomach cavity. The gall stones had to be removed without delay. Finally on March 21st he was admitted to the Schumpert Hospital.

Before laser or computer-aided surgery, surgery was much more intrusive than is the case now. The operation was deemed to be 'extremely challenging' and not without risk. The procedure required the torso to be lacerated around half its circumference. This lasted an incredible eleven hours and, as might be expected, the period of recovery was hardly an overnight affair. Amazingly, John was allowed to go home on March 27th and Michelle was thrilled to see her daddy, although he was, of course, frail after his appalling ordeal.

Meanwhile, I was kept busy thanking friends and neighbours for their marvellous support. I soon settled back into family routine and the presumption that all would be well from here on. The healing process for John did, however, take a very long time. This was only to be expected as it was a long and very challenging operation. We also needed to consider John's diet, which was quite pernickety.

It had not been the best of years for John. I also had to cope with his occasional bouts of depression. This left me little choice but to face up to the fact that he was not in the best of health and he was unlikely to fully recover. His drinking increased again, as he was soon back to prolonged socialising at the Petroleum Club.

Otherwise, all seemed good with the outside world. On June 6th the Suez Canal was re-opened. This was a big relief for a world dependent upon east of Suez oil.

Dad arrived in June for a visit. It had been a long haul for him: Pan Am to Houston and then a flight to Shreveport. On arrival, Dad looked fit and soon settled down as we took ourselves off to Sansome's Rest, where after dinner, we danced in the Continental Room.

John was flying a lot and occasionally taking one-day return trips to Houston. We enjoyed the company of friends and loved to go swimming. Michelle had taken to water sports like a duck.

On July 16th the Inland Revenue Service, seemingly at random, picked on us to be audited.

I was kept busy running things at our home. There was far more for me to attend to than the domestic tasks. At the same time, I was dealing with the complexities of various taxes: household insurance, banking, paying bills. These were ongoing and the light at the end of the tunnel never got bigger or brighter.

The chores included paying John's child support to Laverne for their children Kellye and Tami every month. I also took care of our autos by keeping them serviced and topped up with fuel. I shopped, cooked, and each day took Michelle to school and brought her home. John's health was always an issue and his blood pressure was such a worry. This condition had to be monitored and brought down as need be, but his drinking didn't help.

On August 8th John and I went to Houston's Allied Bank to deposit a cheque from James Cunningham. This amounted to $25,000. Smiling, I see I added a note in my diary that it was not enough. I can't recall what my scrawled remark meant. Anyway, the windfall meant we could do some retail therapy, followed by a lovely dinner in the gorgeous courtyard of St. James. We were also able to buy a puppy for Michelle. The pet was promptly named Laddie. Afterwards, I rushed home and settled accounts with dear Mrs Welch for her babysitting Michelle.

I was taking golf lessons at the time. It was during one of the sessions that Laddie managed to wriggle under our garden netting and was free to commit the mortal sin of wandering about the golf course. Thankfully, Lillie, our housekeeper, got Charlie, the greenkeeper, to bring him home.

After a week of canine misdemeanours, it occurred to us that Michelle was too young and immature to be responsible for such a pet. Laddie did go to a good and caring owner, a local boy named Timmy. The youngster offered to pay for Laddie with his earnings from selling grass cuttings, which we denied. What followed was an emotional parting but we had little choice in the matter so we had to be practical.

Our rent was increased to $575 a month and finally we were in a position to purchase our home from Durward for the initial asking price of $70,000.

There were many other things to deal with and I discussed the prospect of Sandy taking custody of Michelle should anything untoward happen to John and me. We discussed such an eventuality and she agreed that she would be happy to take care of our daughter for a month or so if necessary.

After I ended my seventh golfing lesson, my coach Oran Wittington said, 'I will set you loose now.' So off I sallied to the golf store where I purchased a complete set of clubs. Not being knowledgeable, my purchase was a set specifically designed for top golfing professionals. No one thought to tell me that. The purchase set our accounts back by $175 plus the $27.50 I paid for my new golfing shoes.

John found it necessary to make yet another trip to Houston. By now he knew the route so well he could have flown his own aircraft. Arriving there he met Buddy Williams, the ex-McCulloch executive, and that evening the two went to Fred Parker's home.

Back at our home in Shreveport, Michelle was getting one childhood illness after another. On this occasion it was chicken pox. And thank you, I contracted it too.

Then, I received a long and lovely letter from Connie Boryer, John B's mother and Stefanie's grandmother. She had just met her granddaughter for the first time. I wrote a long letter back and included photographs taken while she was staying with us. Previous to this, I had only one small photo of Stefanie. This was taken when she was twelve-years old and had been published in a local newspaper as a consequence of her having taken part in a stage production at school. The photo of her was so endearing, I carried it with me everywhere I went. Later, Stefanie wrote and said she had taken up secretarial work as a temp in London. Following in my footsteps perhaps? Also she had got back together with her boyfriend, Chris.

CHAPTER NINETEEN
HEALTH AND OTHER ISSUES

DECEMBER WASN'T a good time for John, and by association, it wasn't a good time for me either. John was very sick and contracted influenza and I too picked it up. Happy Christmas indeed! On December 31st John drew a line under his job and handed in his resignation to James Cunningham.

There was some emotional turmoil as neither of us knew what would happen next. There were promising deals that needed scrutinising. John was frantically scooting all over North America chasing leads, but his search proved fruitless.

John's health was also a matter of constant concern. Our hectic lifestyle, plus the worry and need for a settled position, was very unsettling. The only break in our dismal existence was a two-day trip to Los Angeles to see Sandy's daughter, Erin.

February 26th was Michelle's birthday. Mrs Neal crafted a beautiful birthday cake for Michelle, who was the 'grand old age' of four years. Then there was her birthday party at Hamills Park, which had a clown theme and was a great day for everyone.

Michelle was attending Bible classes with Mrs Welch and she also had ballet classes. For my part, I had my ceramics classes to keep me occupied and help satisfy my need for creativity.

On July 14th, my dad arrived and I must say I was so pleased at his appearance. Dad was obviously very good at looking after himself. John took Dad to the Petroleum Club and both benefited from the visit. There are many such clubs in 'oil towns' such as Houston, Denver, Midland, Dallas, Fort Worth and Oklahoma City. All were downtown and easy to reach from airports. The Petroleum Club was fitted out like a London gentleman's club with much teak and leather furniture of refined taste. Unlike similar clubs in London, lady visitors were allowed but only when accompanied by their husbands or partners.

Many of the deals struck in the oil and petroleum industries found their genesis in such clubs. Every deal made had its beginning in a few drinks and a hearty lunch. I remember being quite impressed by our sharing a table with Bob Six, the then chairman of Continental Oil.

Recovering his old tracks, Dad picked up the phone and chatted with Kellye and Tami in Los Angeles. Both were over the moon on hearing from him. He accompanied Michelle and me to the golf club. Dad was very fond of Michelle and she followed him everywhere. Their zest for life was quite remarkable and, of course, brought enormous pleasure to all who observed their togetherness.

John had to make another round-trip visit to Houston and there he met Tony Mancuso. He was thankfully home in time to enjoy Dad's birthday on August 15th. My father was now seventy-three, but the years had been kind to him.

John was planning a visit to Houston the next day for a meeting with Mr Vandenburgh from AMOCO. That afternoon, John called me and he was slurring. He was drunk and this lapse caused me much concern. However, he was in better shape when he returned the following day. Thank goodness I had my ceramics classes to keep me sane. Dad kept himself busy by attending the Louisiana horse races at The Louisiana Downs. I accompanied him, as well as two other ladies. Lucky Dad!

Wanda went shopping with Michelle and bought her a tricycle and this gift brought her much joy.

John was good at arranging barbecues and his steaks were incomparable. Bob and Wanda would join us at such events that were always held on Saturdays. On Sundays, I sometimes made huge roast beefs with all the trimmings. Dad thoroughly enjoyed these dinners, as indeed did everyone. On this occasion, Dad was able to stay with us for six weeks and every minute was enjoyable. It was always heart-breaking to see him go.

On September 7th Michelle returned to school. She was staying with Mrs Welch while John and I flew Delta to Los Angeles, where we would stay at the Bel Air Hotel. There would be dinner with Don, Sandy and Erin and then back to the hotel's bar, which was sadly closed. Never mind, as there was a bar in each of the hotel rooms, unfortunately!

John's daughter Tami started at Humboldt University. Sonia Chernus called regarding *The Other Side of Midnight*, a film then being cast by my friend, English director Charles Jarrott, at Fox Studios. I called him and it was a very sweet conversation, but it was too late as the cast was by now completed. This included Jim Beck, Susan Sarandon, and Marie France Pissier.

On 29th September 1976, John took us all out to dine at Firenze Restaurant, Vincent Campanella's place. Beforehand, John and Michelle had gone shopping with the intention of buying me a gold bracelet. It was a very simple and much pleasing piece of jewellery that I really appreciated and wore for years. Michelle wore her lovely red dress and the party ended with the most delightful birthday cakes I had ever set my eyes upon.

John's check-up at his doctor went well, but the parting shot was that he was instructed to lose weight. It was good advice as my husband weighed in at 195lbs. John was becoming depressed due to business matters not working out too well for him. Sadly, such was his depression that he often talked of taking his own life by shooting himself. It was an awful period and I recall spending evenings talking and supporting him.

I was kept busy making a ceramic dog for Christmas and also made a Yule log. If nothing else, my interest kept my mind off what else was happening. Writing Christmas cards was another distraction that helped me through these trying times. Michelle had so many toys such as the Green Machine to keep her occupied, and there was also the school party to attend.

Thus ended an eventful year, with some high moments, often eclipsed by periods of distress. There were so many concerns and much uncertainty about our future.

A few months later, we sadly sold the house on Red Oak Lane and moved back to Houston in search for work for John. We rented an apartment on Augusta Drive and there began the worst part of our life together.

CHAPTER TWENTY
HOUSTON / AUGUSTA DRIVE

DURING MY final year with John in Augusta Drive I underwent many tests at the Houston Heights Hospital. Yes, I was eating well, but everything went through me and added not an ounce to my weight. It was very disconcerting and, on a personal level, alarming. I suffered from constant diarrhoea and it was thought amoebic dysentery was the underlying reason. Then, in the final analysis, it seemed like a eureka moment when the doctor told me, 'It isn't what you are eating, Jill. It's what is eating you.'

This was the last straw and I simply broke down and wept uncontrollably. I realised then that they were right. I called The Samaritans and they put me on to Al-Anon (an association for the spouses of alcoholics).

Come to our meeting on Monday the kindly voice of Mary on the other end said invitingly. I took up her suggestion and, in doing so, turned my life around. Here with Al-Anon, I found myself in a support group all caught up in the same problems, friends who understood and sympathised with my never-ending plight.

The first uplifting sensation was the feel-good factor when you realise that you are not as alone as you think you are. These were warm-hearted supportive people I could relate to and talk with. Some were to become lifelong friends.

From there on, I picked up the threads of my torn life and I pulled myself together. I began to learn how to cope with life married to an alcoholic. I needed to learn how to be detached from a problem that was basically not mine. First, there was a begrudged acceptance that there was nothing I could do to change John. How often I had turned restlessly in my bed thinking about ways I might get the better of the demons that possessed him. There was nothing I had tried that hadn't already been tried by others; they had failed just as I had done.

It was no good hiding the bottles and the cans from him. It was useless to water the alcohol down. I tried one ruse after another but failed. I was fighting a battle that I couldn't win. It was the frustration and the futility of it that had made me so ill that I was literally wasting away. I was consumed by a problem not of my own making. Alcoholism claims not just the victim but his or her family and friends too.

All you can do is watch and whimper as victims of alcohol abuse self-destroy. It is possible but only when they hit the buffers that they may be brought up sharp to realise the 'I can handle it' deceits have been self-delusional. Only at this point is there possibility of their facing up to the problem and to deal or to die with it.

The bottom line is the initiative has to be theirs. There is nothing that family or friends can do to resolve the problem. Cast by fate to be miserable spectators, family and friends can only hope and pray for a successful outcome. This is what I learned at Al-Anon. If nothing else, I felt liberated and reasoned that I was on my way back to health.

It is a horrible truth to come to terms with, but when you do so, it is in a sense liberating. I felt an amazing sense of relief on realising that I was not responsible, that John's condition was not my fault. This for me was the true value of Al-Anon.

We learn there that the recovery process takes in seven slogans:

1) Let go and let God.
2) Easy does it.
3) Live and let live.
4) First things first.
5) One day at a time.
6) Keep it simple.
7) Think listen and learn.

These seven slogans became something of a mantra for me. To start with every day in the shower, I would make myself repeat them. Gradually, I adopted a new routine. It was essential for me to be understanding, sympathetic and kind but *detached*. I learned to use phrases like, 'I am sorry you see it that way,' or 'I am sorry you feel that way.' Then when something said was offensive I could respond by saying, 'That is unacceptable behaviour.' In other words, I learned to detach emotionally. My wonderful sponsor, Mary was such a great friend for many years after.

I went through these seven slogans until the day I found myself saying to John, 'Would you mind leaving this house; you really do need somewhere else to live.' This had to be said unemotionally in a detached and very firm, but calm way, so that they know there is no argument here.

These were difficult words for me to say but I had steeled myself to utter them. I did so, and you know, it actually had the desired effect. He did go and find a flat for himself and a few months later we divorced.

CHAPTER TWENTY-ONE
BACK IN BEVERLY HILLS

WHEN WE left Houston I had split the money in the banks, which was $34,000, with John. I took $17,000 with me. This meant Michelle and I had enough to live on for about one year without an extra income. During this time, I would brush up on my typing and shorthand skills, which I hadn't used for years. Other skills I had since added to my secretarial CV, having managed the finances and taxes for the Wyoming Transport and Trading Company.

Michelle and I flew back to Los Angeles, while my Fleetwood Brougham Cadillac went on our moving truck with our furniture. By this time, I was so exhausted that I could never have driven our car. Besides, I was never very good at long distance driving; I had only ever made one long trip during which I was accompanied by my Yorkshire Terrier Muffin. Then, I had driven from Dallas, Texas to Topeka, Kansas where I had met John at Jack Shortall's friends' home.

That was when I first discovered that long very straight stretches of road have a hypnotic effect on the driver. This condition led to drowsiness, even at times of the day when one would not normally feel sleepy. This meant unintended catnaps en route all of which added up to delay the journey. I decided then that long distance driving was just not for me.

We were met that day at Los Angeles by Don, Sandy, Erin and Bobby whereupon we went on to their home on North Rodeo Drive 507. It was such a relief to be 'home' again. It seemed to make all that had gone before worthwhile. The next day, after the early morning's tedium was completed, we lunched at The Jonathan's Club, at the beach not far from Santa Monica. Meanwhile, Miche and Erin took themselves off to have a swim.

There were still loose ends, so I called Dad and brought him up-to-date with my news. Again, these were moments to treasure. Dad was so happy for me and hung on my every word. With much more to do, I opened a bank account at the Bank of America with my savings. The day was completed with a trip to an AL-ANON meeting which was being held in a Presbyterian church room next door to Sandy's house and could not have been more convenient. I was now chairing some Al-Anon meetings, which I needed to do twice each week.

Otherwise, I wasn't at all myself, and even the occasional glass of white wine was lacking its attraction. Was I showing my age, for the wine had been replaced by decaffeinated coffee and cheesecake? I just was not interested in drinks at all, after all the miseries it had brought to me. Divorce changes everything. Women who were formerly friends now viewed me with caution if not a natural suspicion as a rival. After the divorce, there was the realisation that nothing would be the same again. I no longer fitted in and this provoked a feeling of isolation and loneliness. This is especially so when during one's married life one's social circle of friends was almost exclusively that of other happy couples.

Sandy was truly a wonderful and understanding friend. Michelle and I stayed at Sandy's for the full week, after which the truck carrying our Cadillac and furniture arrived from Houston. Finally, we could move to our flat, 202, 272, South Rexford Drive, Beverly Hills.

My recollection is of being surrounded by six-foot high columns of boxes all towering over my diminutive figure. It seemed that every available space was occupied. Everywhere possible and impossible had been commandeered by the need to put everything in its new home including an exhausted Jill and Michelle.

Another problem was encountered when my eyes settled on some baby cockroaches. The significance of the discovery didn't immediately dawn. At the time I had so much else on my mind, including a cheque for $3,264 received from Houston's Galleria Bank which was Michelle's savings. This went into an account for her at the Bank of America in Beverley Hills.

Time swept on by, as it does when one is busy and distracted. I began to meet my new neighbours. One of them was a film producer. He was hardly MGM, as he was focused on small independently produced films, but he was well enough established to need a secretary. I ticked all the boxes and I made a start with him at an agreed $800 per month.

It was a difficult job as being neighbours it seemed I was always on call. This meant him dropping by when I had other chores to attend to. Asking me to attend to some typing or other task wasn't acceptable and was an intrusion I could do without. A further complication was his partner's dislike for me, which she did little to disguise. For these two compelling reasons, our relationship was destined to be short-lived. We had a talk and settled up. It was the right decision as I later discovered that he had hired and fired two other secretaries who had experienced similar problems.

Meanwhile, Sandy and I got our two heads together and finalised our plans for a trip to Lake Tahoe where my friend had rented a condo. Taking a week off, we took our flight to Reno accompanied by Michelle, Erin, Bobby, and Sandy's maid Tina. There we had such fun and did much swimming and of course enjoyed the pool slide. Such revelry was followed by a dinner party with our friends, Bob, Don's brother and Dorothy and their family. The rest of the evening was chill time and the hours pleasantly passed by as we turned our attention to party games.

A good night's rest restored our zest for life and the next day our little group became a large one. There was even more revelry after our being joined by Doctor Bob's son, Pat, and his wife and children. I did a headcount and seem to recall that we were nineteen of us in number.

The guests were further added to by the arrival of John's youngest, Tami, joining us at our condo. The day wore on with breaks for snacks, and afterwards there was a splendid choice of refreshment. After an entertaining week filled with fun and friendship, and unaffected by the cold of the Lake Tahoe region, we caught our flights back to the warmer climes of Los Angeles. My one regret is that, life having its own agenda, I never was to return to beautiful Lake Tahoe.

Soon after my return, my knees were once again tucked under a secretarial desk. This time, I was employed by Marvin Friedman's real estate company located in Beverley Hills. My job position was situated in reception. This area was a large office where twelve brokers' desks were placed. As these associates were usually out and about with their clients, their desks were largely inactive and I had the place to myself. Throughout the day I typed up listings, which was a particularly tedious job. This depressing situation wasn't helped by my entering a period of vulnerability. Looking back, I realise just how depressed I was during this time. This was a condition not in keeping with my natural exuberance and enthusiasm for life. I resigned after a few months and felt much better for it.

There were other chores to attend to; a mother's work is never done. Our new home was located across the road from the playground of my daughter's new Beverly Vista School. 262 South Rexford Drive had been a positive move. Michelle was now doing well at school, where she has many good friends including a very special one called Jessica. Otherwise, Michelle felt something of a misfit. So many at the school were Jewish, which Michelle wasn't, and many of the other students picked on her for this difference. It was likewise in Houston where Michelle first went to Duschene Academy. This school was very Catholic and so again she was made to feel something of an outsider. Things improved when my daughter went to another Houston school, the Southern Baptist. There she had a very good and friendly teacher, Mrs Ragland, which was much better for her.

Only when we had packed, unpacked and found a home for everything did we realise what a nice home we had. Sure our latest home was compact but it was ideal for our lifestyle's needs now. Michelle got the one bedroom. For my own needs, I turned our living room into a bedsit and this suited me fine with my desk and bookcase.

The problem of the cockroaches was unearthed when I discovered their hideaway inside the bathroom cabinet. This was where I found to my horror a cockroach nest and about one hundred or so baby ones!

Only on further investigation did we realise the cause of the cockroach problem. Each floor of the apartments had its own garbage chute. Anything tossed into it flew down the chute and ended up in the huge tip situated in the block's spacious garage. It was a heaving mass of cockroaches enjoying an endless feast. This appalling situation was common in Beverly Hills and in the fashionable communities south of Wiltshire Boulevard! We dealt with the problem as well as we could.

I did manage to qualify for another position and was hired as a secretary by a top lawyer in Century City. His spacious and impressively furnished office was situated on the top floor of one of two triangular buildings. This imposing building was an architectural talking point so it was quite a good professional position. My employer was a very charming and attractive gentleman. But it has to be said that my office was a tiny triangular-shaped room. The room had a barn door type of entrance and it housed a potted plant; there was the standard desk and seat plus typewriter. My job was to laboriously work on typing legal briefs through each eight-hour day. My goodness, how eight hours could seem like sixteen-hours. But, of course, I was receiving pay only for the eight hours and not what they seemed to be!

This job was simply not for Jill. It was far too claustrophobic, tedious and monotonous. Carrying on would have killed me. So, despite the status of my employer, a great salary, free parking and health insurance, I felt I had to turn my hand in. This was the last job offer I received in Beverly Hills.

I knew my health had drawn the short straw for I had by now lost about fourteen pounds, which is a serious amount for someone as tiny as I was. This angst was entirely due to my terrible experiences with John up to and through our painful divorce. I was little more than a clothes hanger and I was down to a rib revealing eighty pounds (36 kg) in weight. Even so, I was genuinely trying to eat well and recover.

CHAPTER TWENTY-TWO
AN AUSPICIOUS MEETING

MICHELLE AND I muddled on until my birthday, when John arrived in Los Angeles. Soon after we met him, John took us both to the Beverley Hills Hotel Restaurant. The dinner event was very pleasant and filled with fond recollections, with much small talk and pleasantries. When suddenly, from a distant part of the dining room, in strolled a tiny blondish lady. Getting on in years, she was assisted by crutches and on reaching our table the elderly lady paused before speaking.

'Excuse me,' she said. 'My husband has been looking at you all evening and he is wondering who you are.'

Although completely taken aback at her directness, I introduced our party to our visitor. Clearly, she was a very sweet and well-educated English lady, a woman of social refinement. I was soon to discover that we had much in common.

Apparently our unexpected visitor had once starred in silent screen movies, including some of Alfred Hitchcock's early pictures. Her husband, who had shown an interest in our small family party, was the well-known merchant banker Henry Tiarks, of the banking house Schroder Wagg situated in the City of London. As we chatted, I learned that they had retired and were now living as gentility in upmarket Marbella, Spain.

From this unexpected interlude to our dinner event came an invitation for me to take tea with the couple the next day in the hotel where they were staying. Then, after renewed introductions, we took refreshments by the swimming pool. I was transparent about my past and I brought into our chat the social difficulties of being single while trying to cope with raising a child on my own. I was frank about my situation and explained that I didn't have an income. I added that I was finding it difficult to make ends meet. Then, for good measure, I told the couple that I found my future daunting to say the least.

'You are driving into a cul-de-sac, my dear,' Henry said, smiling sympathetically.

There was no debate about that and as we chatted Henry produced a set of photographs. Placing them on my lap, my host explained each image in turn. The photographs were of their lovely home and attractive gardens in Marbella.

'It is perfectly lovely, Henry,' I said with a smile. 'You are indeed very fortunate in life.

Henry smiled somewhat whimsically. 'In appearance only for there is a cloud on our horizon too.'

I was mystified as to how it was possible for such a successful couple who were clearly well-off and socially skilled to find themselves living in an unsatisfactory situation.

Henry motioned his wife not to interrupt. 'You see, Jill. Spain has strict immigration laws that mean being resident for more than one hundred and forty-three days at a time is against immigration protocol. This is imposed for tax-related reasons and my secretary is blackmailing me. It can't continue and she simply has to go. Naturally, I need a competent and straightforward alternative to her.'

'How awful,' I said as I could think of little else to add other than to sympathise with their plight. 'I wish there was something I could do to help.'

Henry smiled. 'But there is something you can do, my dear. I am sure you would love the job.'

'You mean to be your secretary?'

'Yes, of course, my dear.'

On the face of it the chance meeting and now the job offer was manna from heaven. At last, there appeared to be an exit at the end of my cul-de-sac. There was a bonus too. I had told my charming hosts that I had an older daughter who lives in Estepona not too far from Marbella. I explained that she was the owner of a top-class kennels and cattery.

'Then, my dear, you have another reason to come to Spain.' Henry smiled. 'There seems no good reason for you to stay here where you appear to be unsettled and with an uncertain future.'

'I am so tempted,' I said. 'Since I moved to the United States, my English father has become a widower. He often says it is a pity I am living so far away. Many British people have moved to Spain or France. Dad says it would be much easier for him to visit me, and indeed for me to visit him if I lived in Europe. He is more than seventy now.' I smiled with that faraway look in my eyes.

'In which case I think our meeting is fortuitous,' Henry said with a smile. 'There appears to be a situation here that suits us both.'

I could understand Henry's take on things but I could hardly expect him to understand the complexities and dilemmas raised by my relationship with my ex-husband, John. Although I had custody of Michelle, the divorce arrangement stipulated that he was entitled to see our daughter during the summer holidays. The only agreement was John's access to her. I could understand my former husband's feelings if for any reason his rights to Michelle's company were violated.

These considerations had to be weighed against our own well-being and the outcome couldn't be presumed. Undeniably, this was a once in a lifetime opportunity for us both. The more I thought about it, the more I knew in my heart that I couldn't possibly refuse Henry's offer.

Before parting, we shook hands on it and with immediate effect, I started planning our relocation to Spain. There was much to do but the preparatory chores were taken on in good heart and spirit. Again I was selling furniture and other belongings whilst carefully selecting items that I couldn't be parted with. These included my teak desk and bookcase and chair that were purchased in Heal's in London. I determined that whatever the cost these items of much-loved furniture and I were inseparable and would remain with me practical or not. The move from the United States to Spain was to take place nine months after our chance meeting in the Beverley Hills Hotel Restaurant. Throughout this time, I kept in constant touch with Henry and his lady wife. At each step of the arrangements made I kept them in the picture and over time we became close and trusting friends. Finally, we had a date to aim for and this was determined to be June 28th, 1980.

My agreement with John was that Michelle would visit him for summer holidays. He was a bit reluctant but he knew it made sense for us. She did visit him every summer until one when she begged me not to send her over like a sack of potatoes. She explained that there was nothing for her to do there as her dad and his new wife would be drinking most of the time. In response to her not coming, he stopped child support! She took that very personally and I tried to explain it was not meant to hurt her, only me.

CHAPTER TWENTY-THREE
MOVING TO SPAIN

LEAVING THE United States on June 18th 1980, we flew to England, which I had missed in many ways.

Michelle was now seven and we were both excited by this life-changing new adventure. Michelle was trusting and optimistic as most children are. I think it was her trust and confidence that acted as a balm for my own mixed feelings.

After our long flight, we found ourselves back at Cheyham Cottage in East Horsley and under the same roof as Dad. It was our intention to stay with him for a few days and this news delighted him. This was understandable as he was no longer in the first flush of youth and his travelling to the United States had become too draining.

Then on June 28th, after hugs and well wishes, we started our journey to Málaga, a beautiful city located on Spain's Mediterranean coast. On arriving at the airport, we were met by Stefanie, who had come to greet us in her small run-around car.

Oh, the dog hairs were everywhere in evidence, from her kennels and cattery. She was now a country girl and very successful too.

She dropped us off at a flat she had rented on our behalf. It was to prove an inauspicious start. That night, Michelle and I shared a mattress on the floor and awoke to find we had been sleeping it was waterlogged. Using a variety of sponges, mops and buckets we resorted to bailing out our temporary bedroom as the tank had burst. It was distressing and unnerving at the time, but like much else in life the recollection continues to amuse us.

We immediately re-located to another flat and this again was impermanent. Clearly, there was a need to put some time and effort into finding somewhere more satisfactory and enduring.

Our diligence finally paid off when we discovered a beautiful flat in Andalucía del Mar. This we rented and eventually Henri Tiarks purchased it for us. We were to enjoy life there for the next nine years. During this time, I was working with Henry Tiarks as a secretary and administrator in his home office, within a large four-bedroom house which he had built next to the Marbella Club.

As one might expect, he had a few employees. Thanks to my accounting skills I was in touch with Henry's London-based accountants. I used to type up the monthly accounts at my home at the weekend. The trusty typewriter was later replaced by a word processor, the latest thing!

Working with Henry was a wonderful experience and I had become very much a part of the family. Each day we lunched together with his wife on the villa's terrace and afterwards I took a dip in the swimming pool. It was a full and interesting life. Due to my position, I soon became acquainted with the family's circle of friends. It seemed Henry knew everyone in Marbella, many of whom were to visit us and enjoy lunches and swim in the pool occasionally.

Henry Tiarks was well-connected and indeed his associates and friends knew no borders. My employer was a director at Schroders, which is now the merchant bank Schroder Wagg & Co. Henry had been involved in the settlement of Britain's war debt and the signing of the agreement which took place at Lancaster House. He was also involved in the financing of the Antofagasta railway system in Chile. Being of German and English descent, Henry was proficient in both languages and fluent in Spanish too.

At that time, Marbella was much smaller than it is today; the lovely city was also very chic. This was largely due to the presence of the Habsburgs, who were so influential in the building of the Marbella Club. Prince Alfonso Hohenlohe and Count Rudi von Schönberg were close friends of Henry. There was also the Bismarck connection and the friendship of Count Plattenberg, who wanted me to work for him. The count's home was situated across the street from Casa Ina, Henry Tiark's home. I told Henry of the approach and he was displeased, but needless to say I stayed with Henry.

Henry was tough when it came to financial matters, which adversely affected me. Being in Spain without documents left me vulnerable and I was not in a very strong bargaining position. With a little help from Dad, I managed to put Michelle through Calpe College in San Pedro de Alcántara, where she was to be a student for six years. Then her education became a matter of Michelle's choice. My daughter's preference was Hurst Lodge, a boarding school in Berkshire. It was this school where Sarah Ferguson, later the Duchess of York, had been a head girl.

Michelle did very well. Enjoying ballet, she won the school's choreography cup. Being away from Spain was beneficial for her because back in those days the problem of drug-taking was affecting school pupils as young as thirteen or fourteen years of age. Everyone was worried.

Henry Tiarks had also been responsible for the building of many of his houses, and this one where he was now living was about his tenth built home. I assumed house acquisition was an interest of his. My employer had a home in Nassau, with Noel Coward as his neighbour. Later on in the Channel Islands, in Jersey, Henry had built Cardington Lodge, situated on the cliffs.

Henry and his wife Joan also had a house on Abbey Road in London, where the famous Beatles studio is.

Unfortunately, Joan became highly dependent upon Henry following a period of depression. Since I settled in, she had developed the habit of watching old Fred Astaire movies and musicals and the two of us were constantly distracted by her interruptions.

As a consequence, work had become much more difficult. His wife would call him to her bed for his attention with this or that ailment; she felt very alone and unhappy.

We ended up hiring nurses after reading an advertisement in *The Lady* periodical. We interviewed applicants in Spain, but mostly they did not last very long.

As a couple, they really had nothing in common, only their shared social life when they were younger. They had a daughter, whose name was Henrietta, who was Debutante of the Year in the 1960s.

Her daughter wanted most of all to be an actress, but her mother was set against her entering the world of theatre. Henry even arranged for her to meet Walt Disney but Joan was determined to end her daughter's wish to be an actress. Instead, she married the Duke of Bedford's son Robin, who upon his father's death inherited his father's title.

Henrietta had a real flair with horses and they had a large stud farm at Woburn Abbey in Bedfordshire. She even managed to pick a winning foal at birth, named Jupiter, and sent it to Japan, where he won the Japan Cup. Henrietta was then presented to the Japanese emperor.

Henrietta had three sons, Andrew, Michael and James, all of whom were schooled at Eton. Henrietta and Henry argued much and there was a sad triangle with her mother.

For several years Tiarks would talk about writing his book and telling me stories I would need to write. However, it never happened because we were kept busy working on projects needing immediate attention. So I feel glad I can at least say some things about him.

He had one great friend who worked with MI5 in London, and who was helping to write his own book. He would narrate his story to Henry over the phone during the evenings so he could receive some feedback. This was Leo Marks, the famous code breaker. Tiarks wanted me to meet him in London because he thought he might be able to help to find my biological parents, which I had given up as my attempts had always ended up in dead ends.

Apparently, so did his efforts. It was assumed that the failure was due to records being lost during the war years. Anyway, we had a nice lunch at the Chelsea Arts Club. He was married to a portrait painter, who was quite famous. He did get his book completed and published in 1998: *A Code Breaker's War 1944 – 1945 Between Silk and Cyanide.*

Henry Tiarks had many interests even after his retirement, including the World Wildlife Fund and the European Atlantic Group, which involved my secretarial skills. He was also keen on astronomy though he was scornful of my interest in astrology. He even built and copied to the last detail the observatory at Eton College and had made and placed it in his garden in Casa Ina. It was a fantastic telescope. Tiarks was involved with the Malaga Observatory Society. The associates would visit Tiarks in Marbella often to look at the stars in the night sky.

According to Henry's wishes, when he died Count Rudi was to place the telescope in the park of the Constitution in Marbella, where it is today a fine monument to a special man.

Henry Tiarks had two great sayings: when he forgot something, he said he was not absent-minded, it was presence of his mind elsewhere. This was a phrase that Clara Booth Luce of the Washington Post used. And she also used to say 'no good deed goes unpunished'.

Back in 1983, while working as Tiarks secretary, there was a nice celebration when the fluffy white dog belonging to the cook gave birth in the kitchen to five tiny puppies.

The dog had apparently had a liaison with a black-and-white Welsh Border Collie living not far down the street.

It so happened that Michelle was going to be eleven years old on February 26th. When the puppies were six weeks old I choose one and took him home on her birthday and placed him by her bed. When Michelle saw this tiny thing looking up at her, it was love at first sight.

My father christened him Snoopy because he looked like the black-and-white cartoon dog. Dad came to stay with us during the summer. Tiarks invited him to come to work with me and he sat in the garden in the swinging hammock-type seat and read his book. He would then enjoy lunch with us on the terrace and afterwards he would swim in the heated pool with us. When Snoopy got a bit older, he was allowed to be in the pool with Michelle when she was on school holidays.

I had a ground floor flat in Andalucía del Mar, opposite The Andalucia Plaza Hotel and used to let Snoopy out of my French windows into the communal garden. He was a sweet-natured dog and never aggressive but he was very randy. He used to chase the female dogs and was frequently successful in catching them.

Often someone would say in passing, 'Oh, I have a little puppy, which looks just like your dog, Snoopy.' Even Stefanie at her kennels and cattery told me that when she had a Snoopy lookalike and that was in Estepona!

When Michelle was attending Calpe College at San Pedro, she caught the school bus home during the late afternoon. The bus stopped at the entrance of the port., so the parents would all gather for their happy hour in the Shark Bar, while they waited for the bus.

The bar was owned by a large Dutchman named Jan, who owned a Harley-Davidson. The place was filled with all kinds of foreigners, all trying to make a living in Spain. The atmosphere was great and full of fun. One day, while I was waiting for Michelle, a small yacht moored down one of the piers a short walk away from the bar, and who should enter but my dearest college girlfriend from St. James's, Anne Houlbrooke-Bowers, whom I had not seen for over twenty years. She was with her husband Mike and friends. Meeting her and her husband in such circumstances was truly incredible.

We looked at each other, embraced and were almost in shock – then we started chatting exactly where we had left off! It turned out that she and her husband had a house in El Palo on the hillside. They had two children, a boy and a girl. Needless to say, we never lost touch again.

We had a combined sixtieth birthday party and again for her eightieth at her home in the hills overlooking Malaga Bay. Ironically, her daughter and her family bought a house in West Horsley, my parents' house having been in East Horsley in the Surrey countryside.

I was rather lonely when Michelle went to boarding school. I used to walk to Puerto Banus where friends had an evening at a piano bar called Playback. Claude from the Marbella Club would be playing the piano and singing with a guy from Nottingham. Friends sat around and danced on the small dance floor. It was a great atmosphere and we all knew each other. Puerto Banus was like a friendly village back then and totally unspoilt. Now, I would never dare to go there at night.

I didn't have a telephone in my flat. Instead I would walk up to the Andalucía Plaza Hotel where they had a row of telephone kiosks. They would place your call for you and then after your call; you paid at the desk.

CHAPTER TWENTY-FOUR
MY LIFE WITH A NOT-SO-GREAT DANE

I CONTINUED to work for Henry Tiarks. Michelle was now eleven and was attending Calpe College near Marbella. At some point, we met some people living in Puerto Banus on moored boats. One young Dane rather appealed to me. He lived on a motor yacht moored there. The yacht was about eleven metres in length and we became an item. An ex-serviceman, he was quite handsome. We two would meet at the Shark Bar when the school bus returned from her school in Calpe College.

Michelle liked my friend very much and the two got on well together. He had been married before and had a daughter about Michelle's age but he was unable to see her. So he played dad to Michelle and would even take her to school in the mornings. We spent a lot of time on his yacht. Michelle had the forward cabin to herself while we had the use of the double cabin.

We had so much fun. I was going to Tiarks' every day and my friend would spend his time working on his boat or reading. Around about the same time Michelle had acquired Snoopy. One day, we noticed Snoopy had disappeared. We looked everywhere and then saw a crowd of people at the end of the pier. When we got there, we found a man with a fishing net, inside of which was Snoopy as he had fished him out of the water. Thank goodness, he was alive and fine. Snoopy had swum all the way down from the pier to the land; it was quite incredible. From there on, he was a swimmer and as he grew up even Tiarks allowed him to swim in his pool as did my dad when he visited.

Snoopy was a fantastic dog and used to race with Michelle along the beach. Of course, when she went to boarding school, he became my dog and he spent my working hours with me. I tied his lead around the leg of my desk. He was very good but one afternoon he got loose and went off down the lane exploring where he got into trouble. He was found in a neighbour's garden where he had decided to leap in the pool and take a swim. Then he couldn't get out. A net was used in an attempt to fish him out but Snoopy slightly bit his rescuer's hand. There was a big fuss and we had to take the man to the vet for him to receive a tetanus shot, which I had to pay for. He was lovely Welsh Border Collie, without much of a tail and he had very short legs. For a while, life went smoothly and I was happy. My friend and I decided it would be fun to make some money if we used the boat as a charter yacht for tourists taking short tips.

So, we made a couple of trips with a maximum of six people. One day, we set sail with two couples and our engineering friend on the boat. One of the ladies came in stiletto heels, tight skirt and designer bag. We said immediately that she could not board with such an outfit on. Neither she nor her companion had ever been on a boat before. Michelle was on the boat too. I served drinks and canapés. After about an hour, the lady was sick. Michelle used green plastic bags that were useful as sick bags. Then, to cap it all, the engine quit. It became dark and the boat was swaying from side to side. Our paying passengers were all sick and poor Michelle was kept very busy (with the bags).

Our engineer was unable to fix the problem and we had little choice but to put out a mayday signal. We rocked and rocked, fortunately in fairly calm seas for another hour. Then the coastguard from Estepona pulled us into the harbour. That was the end of our chartering venture.

My Danish companion's mother had a house in Benalmadena, which she often visited. We used it at weekends and would swim in the pool.

My dear friend Annie and her husband Michael visited us from El Palo and we all swam there. Even my dad came with us when he visited us in the summer. Life was really pleasant. Then, one mad day, the Dane, Michelle and I got in our car. We drove to Gibraltar and we were married. Our doing so was mainly for Michelle's sake as she really needed a father and she and my partner got on so well together.

But unfortunately, things got bad. I was working while my Danish partner was unemployed. I was paying for everything. He was also a secret drinker, which I had not realised. His drinking was very much a problem and was becoming worse.

I had to attend to everything, including making the family dinner. He would refuse to eat my dinners and shut himself in a small en-suite annexe built for a live-in maid or gardener. There, he would lock the door and his only company was a bottle of vodka.

Things went from bad to worse and Michelle and I returned to our lovely flat. Then one day, Annie called me to tell me that her husband, Mike, had found my husband in the gutter in Malaga. The authorities ensured his return to Denmark where he was treated. He survived with diabetes and liver damage. He lived for five years in a special home situated in Copenhagen. Naturally, I was very sad and it seemed I had jumped from the frying pan into the fire. There must be something about alcoholics that attracted me. Poor Michelle was upset at losing her very good friend.

Earlier on, my Dane had said he would share his money with me – half and half from the sale of the boat. So we had gone to my bank in Marbella and signed documents as to the final settlement of the boat's sale, which was £10,000. We had £5,000 coming to us. But on that day I was without my passport. I foolishly said okay. I trust you to give my £5,000 to me later.

Over the years I completely lost touch with him. It was only during work on the Marbella Film Festival, when I met a man named Preben Anderson and his lady, supporting our film initiative with Alexis de Vila, that I asked how I could get a divorce from an ex who lived in Copenhagen.

He found me a lawyer, who set the process up for me. I went there and I met him. The money in the bank had a due date on it fairly soon. I asked him about it. My Danish husband said he would share it with me, but only if I was to let him come and live with me in my flat.

But I could not go back to the past and I refused his suggestion. I got my divorce for only £200, which was very good. My ex turned up in court and sat across from me and throughout the court procedure, he never stopped staring at me. It was so eerie. The judge said I did not need anything from my Danish ex as I stood to inherit wealth from my father. This was true, so that was fine with me. I was at least free.

I had given him the paper from the bank so he was able to get the money on the date due. Out of curiosity I went there and waited and sure enough, he arrived at the bank on the due date. We spoke again and he refused to give me the agreed £5,000. His condition was the same: he could share only if he could live with me. So we made our final goodbyes.

Many years passed and I was tidying up my finances. I found a bond at Barclays. I could not place it and I noticed it had my old married name on it from when I was with my Danish husband. The sum was for £5,000. And then, I remembered that my Dane had said to me that something was so important in his life, namely Noblesse Oblige. I still cry when I remember this.

CHAPTER TWENTY-FIVE
MOVING ON MAKING FRIENDS

IN THE 1980s, I met a Finnish lady whose name was Kaarina Dahl. She was living in Marbella and designing clothes and was organising fashion shows. We became really great friends. Kaarina was a wonderful character and a lot of fun.

Her marriage to Mr Dahl behind her, she was now seeking someone else. She had two grown daughters, both of whom were beautiful. They visited frequently, especially in the summer.

In the meantime, I began modelling in her shows in various hotels situated along the coast. When she was unwell, I hosted a show for her at the Andalucía Plaza Hotel opposite my flat. I knew the management very well. It was all good fun and I loved doing it.

One year, I went with her for a short trip to London, where she had rented a flat for us near Marble Arch. She was there to buy material for sewing, which she would bargain for in open markets.

She then packed her purchases in her suitcase, which was always overweight. She somehow charmed everyone and would always get her own way. Kaarina had some clever tricks too. I would go out in Puerto Banus with her and her children and we would dance in Old Joy's and other places for hours. It was really wonderful.

One night, she was collecting her car from the car park quite late and there was a man walking in front of her. She said, 'Oh, I like the look of that.' She then walked up to the stranger and pinched his bottom. The two got talking. He was English and they ended up living together in his house located on the way to Estepona. Then finally they got married.

Kaarina was an outrageous flirt but with her newfound partner, she had discovered the one she wanted. Meanwhile back at Tiarks house, things were getting very difficult with his wife, Joan, her old age and her loneliness.

Another cross to bear: Henry himself was getting a bit senile. He had been eighty-years old when I had started working for him in 1980. He was now eighty-nine and forgetting things, such as whether or not he had paid me. He would say it was not so. He would go to the bank and lose money from his pockets, etc. Working with him was becoming very difficult. I was feeling desperate for a break from this routine.

One day, I met an interesting guy at a party. We had a long conversation and he asked if I would like to go to Ibiza with him on his yacht. He was an Englishman who owned several businesses. He had his young daughter with him and was divorced.

He had a crew on the boat but they were just two guys. The yacht was not very big. I think it was about fourteen metres. Well, it was so tempting an offer and I decided to go. As it was the school holidays Michelle accompanied us. Going to the island was an added bonus because Ibiza was where Eileen Allison lived with Carlos and their daughter Lara. They had met Michelle when we first arrived in Spain. It was a marvellous sea trip.

Eileen and Carlos go. Some remembered Eileen's

cooking from the stockpot in Comedy Street opposite the Comedy Theatre in London. Many actors were there too and also at the other haunt called The Black Cat. Those were halcyon days. This trip with my new friend lasted just three days. We had to return because there were storms forecast. Afterwards, I did not see much more of him.

Shortly, after this excursion, I heard there was a film institute in Marbella. I was so desperate to return to my old profession and to my long-lost dreams constantly haunting me. So, I went one day to La Virginia where the film studio was located. There I met the guy organiser, whose name was Alexis de Vilar from Barcelona.

We hit it off very well. Alexis was quite a colourful character and full of ambition. He wanted me to work with him to put on a Marbella Film Festival. I was so excited. This felt right and was just what I needed.

I left Tiarks in 1989 but I trained a friend of mine, whom he liked, to replace me. In a couple of months, I was able to hand everything over to her. She had been working with a yacht broker in Puerto Banus and I knew her well.

Alexis opened an office in El Capricho and we hired a Spanish secretary. I was the advertising manager for our new periodical *Marbella Style*. Unfortunately, there was only one issue published. However, we were a good team spending a lot of time structuring our big project. Unfortunately, it all came a cropper. It was because he wanted forty per cent of the gross profit for himself, but his partners wouldn't agree. Alexis was a deal maker but he was not compromising enough.

We had a few fundraisers and parties with top businesspeople and we found a wonderful venue for the film festival on the Golden Mile in the old Oasis building, part of which still stands, converted now of course. It had been empty for many years.

We were still pressing on in 1992 hoping our difficulties would resolve themselves, but obviously not. Then in 1993, on February 14th, I got a call from Dad. It was urgent. Could I come as he was feeling very sick? So I immediately bought a ticket and flew to London and on to East Horsley. My dad was in a bad way. We had not long ago celebrated his ninetieth birthday on August 15th, 1992.

I had organised a party at the Preston Cross. It was his country club and invited were his Royal British Legion friends and others too. I managed to keep it a secret until the day. It was a marvellous occasion with few worries except that I had told him it was a casual event when he asked me. But everyone turned up in dinner suits and he was a bit upset with me. Dad's ambition was to reach ninety-years of age so overall he was happy.

He was in charge of the ladies' Standard Bearers in the south east region of England. And he was presented to the Queen in Coventry for his many years of work which he started after his retirement from the Union Discount Company situated in the City of London. As a child, I remembered him leaving for the railway station in Cheam each morning and wearing a white stiff-collared shirt and suit in a black Homburg hat which was later replaced by black bowler headwear. He would then walk from London Bridge station across the bridge to his office. Sometimes I would go on the bike to meet him off the train coming home.

After the war he went back to the same office as did all his companions and carried on like it was yesterday! He took me up to London when I was about seven to his office where we watched the Lord Mayor's procession, which was a big trill. Dad had been alone ever since 1971 when Mum passed away so I visited him often and he visited me in America and Spain several times too.

CHAPTER TWENTY-SIX
DAD, KAARINA AND LEO

BACK TO February 1993, just after I arrived to care for my dad on the 14th February, his brother died, and my dad passed away on the 19th February. Sadly, this meant we had two funerals to attend, and to cap it all, Michelle's birthday was on 26th February.

Dad had a wonderful church funeral with female standard-bearers holding their flags to attention at the altar. It was very dramatic. I asked them play to 'Land of Hope and Glory'. I cry just writing this.

It was Dad's best friend from the British Legion, McAlister, who laid a wreath was laid for him. Just as he backed away from the memorial stone, a gust of wind blew and wafted the wreath over to my feet. I was stunned. I could not move. Then McAlister fetched it and replaced it at the monument. Afterwards, I wished so much that I had picked it up and replaced it as I was meant to. Now, Dad comes to me like a gust of wind quite often. I try to interpret its meaning; he comes to give me support when I need it most.

Once, in Puerto Banus, he blew a 2,000 Spanish pesetas note at my feet just as money was a bit short. It was an incredible thing to happen. I feel that he is always with me. He was the greatest dad in the world. I loved him so much.

I was very happy to have Michelle staying with friends in London. She came down to Dad's cottage to be with me on the weekends, and she helped me through this very difficult period. I was very busy winding up Dad's estate and I had the help of my cousin, Malcolm Barlow, who was Dad's trustee. So, with our next-door neighbour, Andrew Cook, we managed to empty the loft. It was filled with silver cups and medals awarded by the Honourable Artillery Company, which were Dad's prizes for 'rifle shooting' competitions.

The HAC asked if I would return them now he had passed away, but I was still in mourning. I could not get my head around parting with such special things. I probably should have agreed because I still have them and they could be of more use to them. They are in two large storage boxes.

We finally sold the bungalow, with its beautiful large garden that was Mum and Dad's great joy. They had always spent their weekends together gardening.

After taxes and probate, etc., I still had a nice sum to invest. I had some marvellous advice from a friend in Luxembourg. I was able to buy shares in Norsk Hydro and a couple of others that gave me enough income to live on now that I was virtually without a job. So, I returned to Spain and my modelling job with Kaarina Dahl.

After her graduation, Michelle returned home to Spain where she had a summer job working at a beach bar two-minutes from our flat. She had many young friends and one in particular, but I found it very difficult to have much influence on her. She decided to move to London with her boyfriend, Giles.

Giles was a writer and had a job with a city newspaper. However, Michelle needed to get a work permit. So, together we went to London and got an appointment with the Home Office. They gave her a work permit, so she was on her own in the world. She had a couple of jobs as a receptionist and then got a very good job with a young advertising company as a media buyer. She did very well and made a lot of friends but did not continue with Giles. Instead, she found a flat in Fulham that she shared with two other girls. This worked well for a while and she became very good at working on the computer. She could see that being very good for her future.

After Dad died, and things had settled a bit, I felt the need for a break. I took Michelle to New York for a few days and it was a wonderful trip and very memorable for both of us. We visited all the famous sights and I took her to the Tavern on the Green where we met an English singer-guitarist who was the son of a friend of mine in London. Michelle caught up with him later back in England, which was nice. We also went to the Broadway Theatre to see Glenda Jackson play Lady Macbeth. We had dinner afterwards with her and her agent, Peter Crouch. This was a lovely event and she had previously written her autograph on a photo for Michelle which read, 'Dear Michelle, school does eventually end.'

We did Fifth Avenue and Trump Tower and had lunch at the Plaza Hotel Oak Bar. We went up the Empire State Building with its forty-eight floors. We then visited the The World Trade Centre and viewed the city from the one hundred and seventh floor. Also, the Museum of Modern Art, where as promised, I bought two books for Doctor Nami, Tiarks' friend, the orthopaedic surgeon and collector of modern art, which he was thrilled to get.

After three days we flew to Houston to meet Michelle's father after many years. He had married but had ended up with a worse alcoholic than he was. She had a terrible accident driving her car to the liquor store. She drove into a bus queue and maimed a mother and daughter, after which she committed suicide – simply so horrifying, what could be worse, poor thing.

John has since moved into a care home and, when I saw

him, he looked very gaunt and thin, with dyed brown hair. But he was very sweet and we had a very nice visit.

Michelle went to lunch with him and enjoyed his company for the last time. In the past, she had visited him during the summer holidays, but she had hated so much how he and his wife had behaved.

Michelle was very good at handling her father's affairs in Houston with the help of my Alanon sponsor, the wonderful Mary Ogden Baker, who gave Michelle the support she needed. She was also benefitting from overriding royalty cheques that were made to her and not to me (ORRI's – overriding royalty interest). These are still on-going a little. I waived all my rights to John's oil mineral rights and the judge had said, 'You are the first woman in Texas who has not claimed mineral rights. Are you serious?'

I replied, 'Yes,' because they would go to Michelle anyway so why not now.

These rights can be very valuable when leases are sold for drilling rights, etc. Anyway, she handled everything and was getting a small regular income from the ORRI's and was learning how to handle the paperwork.

So, after our four-day visit to Houston, we flew on up to Los Angeles and stayed with Sandy on Rodeo Drive after not seeing her for about thirteen-years. We caught up with friends, and even Derek Partridge and his wife Joyce dropped in from his home in Glendale.

It was a lovely social week after which we flew back to London, back to the bungalow and the heavy work of moving.

The last thing to be sold was Dad's little car, which he was obliged to leave out in the driveway after all my luggage from America had arrived during those cold winter mornings when he was scraping the ice off the car windows. He was much inconvenienced by me. I felt awful. Michelle was now back in her flat in Fulham and her job after our summer holidays.

*

I returned to Spain and was doing fashion shows with Kaarina. But I was lonely and uncertain about my future with the film festival not working and there not being much to keep me in Spain. I was looking at possibilities and I was seeing a fair bit of Michelle, which was nice. I tried my hand at film production with a writer friend who had a good story and script. He was the director for the BMW TV commercials.

We formed a company with an agent in Hollywood but it didn't work out. I spent time back at Gerry's, my theatrical club again and I talked to lots of people. I did not have an agent anymore. He had died and I was depressed and unhappy with Dad gone and I felt very much alone and a crossroads in my life.

I used to stay with Michelle in Fulham and we always went for a curry at her local Indian restaurant. I applied for income support but I didn't have an address in London. Meantime, I had rented my flat to a friend who was working in Marbella, but he left it in such a mess and still owing me some money. I told him to go. While visiting London, I had stayed at a friend's flat in Ebury Street, which was nice but a bit too close for comfort and so I returned to Spain and resumed modelling with Kaarina. I got Snoopy out of the kennels. He was fine and it was lovely to see him again. Something, I thought, will turn up as it usually does.

And one day, I was over at Kaarina's flat going through the clothes rack for the next fashion show. Suddenly, she said, there is someone you must meet. His name is Leo and here is his telephone number. She had met him at a Finnish party where he was alone. She thought he was right for me. She was quite a matchmaker.

I said, 'Oh, I can't just call him cold.'

'Yes, you can,' she said over and over. She just would not take no.

So finally I plucked up the courage and I telephoned

one afternoon. He picked up the phone. I started to explain that Kaarina had given me his number, but he interrupted me to say he was just on his way out. He was going to Estepona and he said goodbye.

I was so deflated. I felt completely stupid but the next day, after he had checked me out with Kaarina, he called and apologised. He asked me to join him with Kaarina and Irving, her new husband whom she had met in the car park.

Leo invited us to dinner at Tony Dalli's beautiful restaurant on the Golden Mile. Wow! Leo's voice was really nice and I was so excited. I recall that it was February 2nd, 1996, the day Gene Kelly passed away. I dressed up and arrived at Toni Dalli's. I walked down the huge staircase. At the bottom, there was a man in a burgundy silk jacket and dark green trousers. His hair was a lovely brown colour. He was reading the restaurant's menu board. He turned and I was suddenly so happy. We introduced ourselves and walked into where Kaarina and Irving were already seated.

I proceeded to have the most wonderful evening of my life. It was love at first sight for both of us. They left us early and went home and we carried on to the Marbella Club where we danced and chatted until the small hours. Then we went home to my place and jumped into my bed. I made breakfast the following morning. The telephone rang; it was Kaarina, who wanted to know how we had got on. When I told her, 'Fine, we are just having breakfast,' she was so shocked!

'He should not stay over on the first night,' and so her scolding me continued. I was upset and said I would call her later. She, of all people, was shocked, I couldn't believe it. But she was very much a mother hen.

Then the days, in fact weeks went by so quickly and we didn't spend a day without seeing each other. We slept either at his flat in Pueblo Tranquilo or at mine in Andalucía del Mar. I was meeting his friends and getting to know him and likewise, he was meeting my friends. It was a truly idyllic time. I was then fifty-eight and it just happened that I had a long-term financial plan. I had especially saved money to pay for a facelift. Everything was prepared.

It was already arranged when I told Leo. He was afraid they would ruin my lovely natural face, which he had only just now found. But I went to the Clinica Barragan in Madrid and it all went very well. The experience itself, though, was ghastly experience. I did not expect the body bruising. But in the long term, all was well, and as I recovered, I was very happy and thought it was worthwhile. But Leo never thought it to be necessary, bless him.

Ironically, Michelle had decided that she no longer wanted to live in London. She was hungry to return to her roots but she said she would not leave me until I was happy. Then she flew back to Los Angeles where she was picked up by some friend there and got herself a flat in Beverley Hills on South Maple Drive. She shared with a girlfriend. Having a United States passport, she found work quite quickly, especially due to her computer skills. Michelle was now twenty-four.

After my facelift, Leo met me in Malaga when I arrived home from Madrid. I went with him to Pueblo Tranquilo. He looked after me for two or three days but I was very tired. He was keeping busy doing things for the Finnish Church in Fuengirola, where there were living many Finns, many of whom lived in Los Pacos.

Leo was raising money for the Finnish Church parish meeting hall which was a big thing and where all the Finns gathered socially on many occasions. Leo was responsible for raising funds and eventually a new meeting hall was built. He was also organising golf tournaments in Miraflores to raise money for the church.

He was always very busy, although he had retired in 1991. He had planned to come to Spain to live with his wife, a physiotherapist. She had even packed their things when, just before they were due to leave, she had a fall down a flight of stone stairs and cut her head open. She died in Leo's arms. It was simply terrible and shattering but Leo picked up the pieces and came anyway but alone.

He had in Spain slowly created a good life for himself studying Spanish and singing in the Finnish Choral Society. He was very active and he felt useful. He had many friends from his business life and some otherwise. Gradually, I began to meet them. I got involved in his golf competitions, especially at Miraflores. We would arrive at 8.30am and sign-in each of the arriving players, taking the fees, etc.

Leo would then play too. I would go home and come back in time for the prize-giving. We had lovely prizes donated from the Unibank bank. Leo would deliver a speech and give out the prizes. It was great fun.

We went to church on Sundays at the Finnish church in Fuengirola. I would sing the hymns in the Finnish language, which I had learnt how to pronounce but not the meanings of the words. It was lovely and I really enjoyed it and the Finns are very special. Afterwards, Leo would take the collection home and would count it and afterwards place the money in special bags for the bank deposits on Monday mornings.

We played a lot of golf with Leo teaching me the basics on the driving range. We rescued my golf clubs, which were under my bed in my flat. I had bought them in Shreveport when I had been taking lessons in the East Ridge Country Club, backing on to our garden in Red Oak Lane. The clubs were brand new Titleist clubs and still had their wrappers on their hand grips which had melted to the handles due to the heat in Spain.

They turned out to be professional clubs and were far too difficult for me to use anyway. So Leo bought me a new set. Before, I had never had anyone to play with. Originally, when in Shreveport, I had hoped that John would play with me, but for him it was all business, and at the same time drinking.

This was all in the past now and life was becoming what I had always wished it to be. Leo was the man I had needed all my life but we might not have been right for each other had we met at earlier times. Leo always said, 'The first wife is for children, the second wife for business, and the third for love and companionship; the sharing together.'

My history was a bit different and mixed up but I arrived at the same time and on the same wavelength with Leo. This was truly meant to be a marriage made in heaven. And so began all the wonderful enjoyments of travelling, homemaking and friendships. Friendship is not a trend or a fashion. You cannot get interest on it, or a pension, but it is the best investment of your life.

CHAPTER TWENTY-SEVEN
MARRIAGE TO LEO

WE DECIDED to get married in April 1997. Leo contacted the Finish priest, but he could not perform a church wedding because I could not find my Presbyterian Baptism Certificate so we contacted the British Consul in Gibraltar and provided necessary documents for a civil ceremony. We chose April 21st. We asked Michelle to be the maid of honour and our very good friend Esa Laukka to be Leo's best man.

So we set off for Gibraltar and, of course, it started to rain very heavily! We parked the car in La Linea de la Concepción because of the traffic on the border and we had to walk.

Luckily, Leo had his golf gear in the boot, a large umbrella and one raincoat, which he gave to me to put on over my pale blue suit. But we still arrived soaking wet. The brims from mine and Michelle's hats had gone floppy around our faces and my Balenciaga cream high heels shoes were looking sad. Esa and Miche had to go out and search for flowers for the bride, by which time Esa's burgundy silk suit had changed in colour to dark brown. Also Leo's white silk jacket was ruined and looked like a dripping cleaning rag.

The room we were led to was the registrar's office.

Instead of church bells we had a loud and chiming clock and a large Union Jack standing in the corner, with a beautiful photo of the Queen on the wall behind him.

After the introductions, I placed my camera on the desk, ready for the photos, but firstly it was my turn to read the testimony. Then it was Leo's turn. He started off well, repeating what the magistrate said until he got to the word 'solemnly', which being a Finn, he found it difficult to repeat. Just at that moment my camera started to rewind the film, making a loud whirring sound and we all got the giggles, which we had a job to suppress. Poor Leo! After he had tried three times to say 'solemnly' correctly, the magistrate looked very frustrated, and said, 'Whatever,' which Leo then repeated!

So the ceremony was wound up quickly, and then the magistrate's face lit up. He pointed at the photo of the Queen like a toast and we repeated after him, 'The Queen!' – it seemed especially appropriate since it was her birthday!

After the ceremony, we signed the papers and collected these and thanked the magistrate who was happy to get rid of us. Michelle and I went out first with the umbrella; Esa had borrowed one under which he and Leo huddled together. The next party were coming in and seeing Esa and Leo together they stopped, smiled broadly and said congratulations to them!

To cut a long story short, we stopped at a beach restaurant in La Linea and had a long-awaited glass of Cava and something to eat. Then we drove back to Leo's apartment in Pueblo Tranquilo for a hot shower and I ironed my suit and Leo's trousers. We put on the same clothes, some still a bit damp, the hats still very floppy.

The Finnish priest gave us a blessing in the tiny chapel in Mijas. It is on a hilltop and seats only eighteen people in gold painted seats, and we filled all of them with our friends. It was beautiful. The only problem was when I went to kneel down in front of the priest, the soles of my black Balenciaga shoes had peeled off and looked like huge spiders!

We then had a reception in a lovely upstairs restaurant called The Snug, which we had hired, and then we heard outside Esa performing 'Singin' in the Rain' and dancing like Gene Kelly, while holding his keyboard in the middle of the deserted little square below. It was magical and he came in and played for us, soaking wet again!

It was the most hilarious day and full of joy and happiness that everyone remembers. Esa tells it better to all his Finnish friends, all laughing about Leo's and Jill's wedding!

So began a wonderful and busy life travelling to Finland in the summer and Christmas times – also to the United States, New Zealand and England until eventually we settled in Spain.

We met on February 2nd 1996 and married the following year. Now we have been together every day since then. We celebrated our Silver Wedding Anniversary, which was twenty-five years on April 21st, 2022, and the Queen's 96th birthday.

CHAPTER TWENTY-EIGHT
AUTOGRAPHICA BIRMINGHAM

HILTON METROPOLE Hotel 8-9 May, 2010.

Leo, my manager, and I were invited to attend this two-day event in Birmingham, the Autographica. I was representing *Daleks: Invasion Earth 2150 AD*. There were in attendance over forty other celebrities comprising actors, film stars, Apollo astronauts, sports-people, and World War II veterans including RAF pilots.

I felt it was such a huge honour to be among such marvellous people. It was all very humbling and exciting. It was wonderful to meet people with such fantastic stories to tell and I wish there had been more time to listen to more of them. It was also great to meet old friends in the acting world that I had not seen for thirty and more years. There were new friends too, like Tippi Hedren of the Hitchcock films *The Birds* and *Marnie*, and Chaplin film *The Countess of Hong Kong*. She was the only actress who had been directed by both Hitchcock and Chaplin.

Gerry Griffin and his wife Sandy were extremely interesting. He was the man who masterminded the whole Apollo programme. Now retired, he was an expert in so many other interests, not to mention the many companies he was involved in. He is probably busier now than during his Apollo years, and that is saying something.

Gerry Griffin was very concerned about future the space program and mentioned his disappointment at the scrapping of the Enterprise. There had been so much time and money invested in it but for whatever reasons it couldn't go on. President Barrack Obama has gone forward with the Mars program but other than that there is seemingly no real goal any more.

Gerry feels there is more to do on the moon and that we have to return, adding that we have only just scratched the surface, so to speak. He and his wife were travelling with the astronauts Vance Brand and his wife Beverly, Jim McDivitt and Fred Haise and Ed Gibson. Theirs was quite an awesome group.

Then there was my old friend, Dave Prowse, who I worked with in the '60s. He was now a fitness expert and a body builder and had since opened fitness centres in London. Back then we two worked together doing photography for the advertisements. I was so very tiny and David was a huge, tall and muscular man. The subsequent photos of the two of us together were quite funny in terms of contrast. Dave went on to do many things and one of them was to play the part of Darth Vader in *Star Wars*, for which reason he had been invited to the Autographica. I also met the marvellous actor Leslie Nielsen, who was valiant to be there as he must have been in his eighties now and it is quite a tiring event.

Another personality was Alex Higgins dubbed Hurricane Higgins. Unfortunately, the marvellous snooker champion was now extremely ill as a consequence of throat cancer.

It was lovely to meet beautiful Susannah York, whom I have always admired. And it was great also to find that in real life she was also a really sweet person.

Then there was a charming man who came up to my table and started to tell me his story. He was WWII bomber pilot who had been shot down over Holland and taken in by underground fighters. But after about a month in hiding the Gestapo found him. He then went through a hellish time in confinement, followed by interrogation. He somehow survived to tell the tale.

He now looked pretty healthy and walked well for a man well into his eighties. The former RAF man put his navy blazer on later in the event, and I got to see his many medals and ribbons.

There were quite a number of these marvellous and courageous men present. Obviously, they all enjoyed meeting each other and sharing their memories.

Among the actors there were George Baker, best known for his role as Chief Inspector Reg Wexford on the Rendell Mysteries. He also played parts in other roles including *Moonraker* and *The Spy Who loved Me*. Reg was very special and he and Leo hit it off at the Gala Dinner, discussing the merits of Alborg Jubileum among other mutual things.

It was good to see Gerald Harper again from the *Adam Adamant* days back in 1967, and better still to then discover that he was almost a neighbour now and living only a few kilometres away from our home in Sotogrande. Then it was nice to see Ray Lonnen as I had not met him since 1968 in Market in Honey Lane.

Altogether, this was really an amazing international event. That was not just the public's point of view but the consensus of the participants. It is hard to imagine such a varied and spontaneous situation for everyone to meet each other and listen to all their incredible experiences over such turbulent times and amazing lives. We felt we really needed so much more time as two days were not enough, especially as we were all very busy autographing most of the time, which is what we were there for.

But it is a memory which we will all savour vividly for the rest of our lives. From a performer's point of view, Nigel Planer said, 'We Actors only played these different and dangerous roles but here in this hall are the people who did these things for real. They are the real heroes.'

I thought this was a wonderful observation, and it was very humbling. I felt I was certainly honoured to have been asked to take part in this wonderful gala. I give many thanks to Derek Hambly and Caroline and all the team who looked after me, not forgetting Mike and Aidan, who took care of me on the two days. It was very well organised down to the very last detail.

~ Sincerely, JILL CURZON.

MY TRIBUTE TO LEO

LEO GAVE me great support and encouragement with my book, and for several years in the off season we took a week off in March and October from our home in Marbella and stayed at the Hurricane Hotel in Tarifa. There we wrote our memoirs separately as it was quiet and we did not have to do any housework or cook meals. Leo's grandson, Amos, has since typed up Leo's memoirs and I shall have to get them translated of course.

Leo has suffered so much in the last few years. He was in hemodialysis for nearly five years, twice a week from the loss of his kidneys due to diabetes. And his mobility and strength became less and less, and eventually he had to use a wheelchair.

Then, last summer, we were in Finland visiting his cousin for her ninety-ninth birthday, and during the joyful event Leo had a nasty fall, breaking his hip, which was quickly fixed with two titanium screws. But he then spent two months in hospital.

So I went home and prepared the necessary alterations to the house ready for his return on October 27th. He was so brave and stayed positive and worked hard trying all kinds of exercise programs to strengthen his legs, but to no avail.

And then one night, I told him that my book was finally finished and he smiled happily and went to sleep.

In the morning he looked so peaceful, but sadly he had gone to a better place. I had to be happy for him, but was and I still am, devastated and alone.

We had a really wonderful life together with many friends. He loved to cook for and we travelled a great deal to America, Australia and New Zealand.

He was the dearest person I ever met, with all the great qualities a man could ever have. Everybody loved him, especially his three children and eight grandchildren.

I am hoping to write another book about our life together following this one, if I am still here.

Your loving wife, Jill.

CREDITS

FILMS

1963
80,000 SUSPECTS (Rank Organisation). Directed by Val Guest. Starring Claire Bloom and Richard Johnson. I played the role of Julie.

1963
DR. SYN (Walt Disney). Directed by James Neilson. Starred with Patrick McGoohan, Michael Hordern and Eric Flynn.

1964
SMOKESCREEN (Rank Organisation). Directed by James O'Connelly. Also the part of Julie (cockney).

1964
INTELLIGENCE MEN (Rank Organisation). Directed by Bob Asher. Starring Morecambe and Wise. The part of Francoise, a French whore.

1966
DALEKS' INVASION EARTH 2150 A.D. (British Lion). Directed by Gordon Fleming. Starring Peter Cushing and Bernard Cribbins.

1966
MAGNIFICENT TWO (Rank Organisation). Directed by Cliff Owen. Starring Morecambe and Wise. Also, the part of Women's Army Sergeant.

1967
I was also in Clay Pigeon Shooting Films for Pathe Pictorial and Imperial Metal Industries of Great Britain.

THEATRE

1962
REPERTORY THE PENGUIN PLAYERS Summer Season in Tunbridge Wells, Hastings, Eastbourne, Brighton, Blackpool and Bristol.

1964
PHOENIX theatre in London west end – MONSIEUR BLAISE starring Jimmy Thompson. Ran for six months. I played the part of Pepita, a Spanish girl and spoke entirely in Spanish.

1969
U.S.A. ROBERTA a Jerome Kern production starring Bob Hope and filmed in Dallas for NBC.

COMMERCIALS Over twenty-five commercials shot in Europe doing voice work, dubbing, on camera, etc.

FILMS US HOLLYWOOD

1968
SUNSHINE PATRIOT with Cliff Robertson and Dina Merrill.

Directed by Joseph Sargent. Producer Joel Rogosin of Universal.

1969
IT TAKES A THIEF with Robert Wagner, directed by Alan Reisner. Producer Jack Arnold of Universal.

BBC

1962
JUKE BOX JURY with David Jacobs as a celebrity guest.
1963
POINTS OF VIEW with Robert Robinson.

1962-1964
HUGH & I the comedy series and a leading role for three series playing the part of the cockney girl named Norma.

1965
TERRY SCOTT SHOW a comedy special (*Scott on Birds*). I was the Bride Bird.

1965
NOT ONLY BUT ALSO starring Peter Cooke and Dudley Moore. I made two appearances.

1965
HUDD. A comedy series. I made two appearances.

1965
THE WORLD OF WOOSTER starring Ian Carmichael and Dennis Price, the award-winning comedy series by P. G. Wodehouse. I played the part of Gwladys, the mad artist. Directed by Michael Mills.

1966
QUICK BEFORE THEY CATCH US. A guest role in one of the four part stories that the series was comprised of.

1966
LATE NIGHT LINE UP. A discussion programme and chat show as a guest.

1967
THE CHAMPIONS directed by Don Sharpe. I played the part of an airline hostess.

1967
MORECAMBE AND WISE
PICCADILLY PALACE – Comedy special starring Morecambe and Wise. There were several appearances in comedy and character roles.

1967
ADAM ADAMANT starring Gerald Harper and playing the part of a Spanish dancer.

1967
The **DICK EMERY SHOW** the famous and highly popular comedy playing the part of the cockney secretary.

1967
DEE TIME with celebrity guest Simon Dee.

INDEPENDENT TELEVISION

1962
OUT OF THIS WORLD a drama series titled THE TYCOONS playing the part of the playgirl, Bubbles.

1965
MRS QUILLEY'S MURDER SHOES. Play of the Week starring Mile O'Shea and directed by Peter Collinson as the Cockney girlfriend, Vera.

1965
THE SAINT starring Roger Moore. As a guest playing the role of Italian girl Maria Cavallini.

1965
RIVIERA POLICE the drama series with guest star billing and shot on location in London and Nice with John Mellon.

1965
ROAD SAFETY FILM produced by Random Film Prods, the producer being Shirley Cobham.

1966
THE LATE-NIGHT LINE-UP a talk show which incorporated interviews, live music and poetry performances and discussions.

1966
ARTHUR HAYNES the comedy series as the girlfriend.

1967
DES O'CONNOR SHOW, the popular comedy with various sketches and characterisations.

1967
PETTY COAT LINE UP hosting female chat show.

1967
ON THE BRADEN BEAT the late-night variety show as a guest part.

1967
CARNIVAL TIME with Pete Murray, Bob Monkhouse and directed by John Paddy Carstairs.

1967
THE DAVE ALLEN SHOW' an ATV production directed by Gordon Reece.

1968
MARKET IN HONEY LANE starring John Bennett in which I played the part of Spanish au-pair.

ACKNOWLEDGEMENTS

Enormous thanks to the marvellous Laura De Witte, without whom I would never have got it all together.

Peter Sims, my agent whose care and enthusiasm and continued encouragement spurred me on when I needed it. And also his good partner Andrew Boyle, and the rest of the team: Scott Mason, Joanne Cameron, Trevor Dobbin and Ray Warren. All of whom helped me with the photo shoot with the Dalek at the recent *Doctor Who* event in Crawley.

Tom Connor from 'Tom's Refurbishments' and Dean Stoner was the Dalek provider for the photo shoot.

And many many thanks to Derek Humbly and his wife Caroline who became good friends over the years starting with his shop 'The 10th Planet' in Barking.

He timed that one to fit with the opening of the new shopping mall so we had a queue to my signing, which stretched around the whole gallery of the mall.

And Shaun Russell at Candy Jar Books who believed in me.